THROUGH THE VEILS OF MORNING

An Inner Journey in the Pathways of Francis and Clare of Assisi

Liam Francis Costello OFM

VERITAS

First published 2000 by
Veritas Publications
7/8 Lower Abbey Street
Dublin 1

Copyright © Liam Francis Costello, 2000

ISBN 1 85390 500 3

British Library Cataloguing
in Publication Data.
A catalogue record for
this book is available
from the British Library.

Cover design by Lucia Happel
Printed in the Republic of Ireland by Betaprint Ltd, Dublin

He gleamed like a shining star
in the darkness of night
and like the morning
spread over the darkness.

– Brother Thomas of Celano

CONTENTS

PREFACE

At the dawn of the third millennium, age-old questions arise: 'Who am I?' 'Who are we?' 'What is the meaning of life?' Many centuries ago, Francis and Clare of Assisi faced those questions and, led by the Spirit, found a pathway that brought joy and hope to their lives. Francis, at the end of his life, could say, 'I have done my part, may the Lord teach you yours'. Francis and Clare lived in the thirteenth century – a time of great change. They have much to say to us today as we enter the third millennium.

In presenting the events in the lives of Francis and Clare that shaped their responses to those important questions, I hope that you will find your pathway. In establishing these guidelines, I am grateful to Professor Michael Guinan, OFM, and Professor William Short, OFM, of the Franciscan School of Theology, Berkeley, for their guidance and help. I thank my Brothers and Sisters of the Franciscan Family in Ireland, and many friends for their help and encouragement. I thank Veritas, my publishers, the production manager in Veritas, Maura Hyland and in particular the general editor, Aideen Quigley, for her patience, help and advice.

I hope that these signposts will help you to discover the pathway that meant so much for Francis and Clare and that, like them, you will lead many on that road.

Liam Costello
January 2000

INTRODUCTION

ABUNDANCE OF LIFE

The Way of Joy

Musicals, fairy tales and stories have been written with happy endings. Many of them follow the fortunes of very poor people who eventually discover that they have always been, unknowingly, heirs and heiresses to unlimited wealth. Today we often view such stories as mere fantasy, yet from time to time they rejuvenate us with their liveliness and simplicity.

To begin what is to be our special journey, we assert that our dream *is* reality for you and for me, with the promise of discovering that our inheritance is not illusion but a firm guarantee, which, when grasped, is the source of great joy.

Simply put, that is what the Good News is all about, and this is the content of faith – acceptance of the dream and the promise. To live on this basis is to discover what reality is, and equally, to discover that the many things we think to be solid, firm and lasting are but illusions. People who come together in Christ to explore and discover creatively will find the hidden source of joy, no matter what their circumstances.

God's Agenda

Life is with us, life has a meaning, and life can be joy. Rather than try to discover this truth and help others in the journey, we generally accept our own created meanings of life, based on comforts, securities and conditional liaisons. Often we can name *our* solutions and call them definite and concrete pathways to happiness. We can title them under the name of religion, culture or even God. God can be falsely imaged in different cultures and traditions, be it Christian, Jewish,

Hindu, Muslim, Buddhist, etc. For Francis and Clare, this could at times represent the 'golden calf' to be destroyed (Deut 9:7-21). Their desire and love for freedom, their love of that royal generosity manifested in the God who was revealed to us in Jesus, as well as their pathway, which they called poverty, separated them from the slavery that engulfs all who live lives based on illusion, on things that cannot last.

The true God values us, particularly when we are naked and vulnerable. To be truly human is to transcend one's heredity, one's environment, just as Jesus transcended his, and as Francis and Clare transcended the Catholicism of their time. Transcendence involves going beyond, and seeing all as interrelated in God. For Francis and Clare, that transcendence could be experienced and lived in the present. There are many routes to the discovery of God. The way of Francis and Clare is but one. However, their decisive and radical choices help us see that there is a road we may not yet have risked on our journeys.

Francis and Clare lived at a time of upheaval in society. Their individual decisions, and the risks they took as they recognised the presence and voice of their Creator in the circumstances and events of their lives, and also in the signs of their own times, should give us courage also to journey with our own authority.

This book attempts to set out on the pathways taken by both Francis and Clare in their journey to inherit the pearl of great value. Hopefully it will enable us to begin to see their way to this treasure and help us in our own journeys.

The programme is designed primarily for groups of participants in a retreat situation, but I would encourage individuals who may want to follow the programme in their own time to do so. In either case, it is important to bear in mind that Francis believed that the Holy Spirit guided the entire fraternity and, thus, each brother's and sister's life. This supposes that each one is listening to the Spirit. Within the

2

heart of the participant who so listens, the Spirit prompts the awareness of need. The Spirit likewise prompts desires that yearn for fulfilment.

Guidelines for Facilitators of this Process

'The first task of ethics is to help us rightly envision the world.'[1] The constant invitation is to 'come and you will see' (Jn 1:39), and 'You will see greater things than this' (Jn 1:50). Many look back and see providence in their lives, a pattern, not just chaos or chance.

In a Franciscan context (in fact, in any prayer-filled context), openness to the Spirit suggests allowing participants to determine for themselves when and with what frequency they meet with the facilitator. In Francis' Rule for Hermitages, the dynamic is this: the 'son' seeks out the 'mother' when in need.

Whether or not a participant actually experiences anything in a sensible or perceivable manner is God's business. It is not uncommon that participants experience nothing. This is more likely to occur in people who are faithful to personal meditative prayer on a regular (usually daily) basis. Thus, it becomes paramount for both participant and facilitator to be attuned to what can be termed 'God's business'.

The role of the facilitator then is simple but demanding: to be fraternal and maternal in nurturing the participants; to be a listener; to be one who accepts participants where they are before God; to be one who encourages an open and receptive heart that waits with patience – a heart that desires to be centred in reality.

Facilitators, therefore, become servant-sisters/brothers, by fostering whatever the group wishes to concentrate on, since the scheduling of what is common should be a matter of consensus. Deep silence of the heart needs to be fostered.

The ethos throughout, on the part of the facilitators, needs to be that of the 'mothers' who are, as it were, nurturing the 'sons'. These terms are Francis' own. He uses them to refer to the style of relationship between the brothers whose call it is to live in hermitages. This spirit also reflects the attitude of service that is so typical of Francis himself. He was the servant of all. As for the brothers, 'they should voluntarily serve and obey one another'; 'they should be the lesser ones, subject to all who are in the same house'. Thus, all participants are facilitators, and all facilitators are participants, nurturers of each other. Any mothers present among the participants will be able to relate to the depth of feeling and to the bond that normally exists between mother and child. A mother will enquire about the welfare of her child especially when her child is in trouble.

Thomas of Celano, in his second Life of the saint, writes that Francis 'not only prayed, but became himself a prayer'[2] inasmuch as prayer was no longer something he did, but something he lived. What he practised, he prescribed for his brothers and sisters.

Francis wrote the following letter to a colleague, Leo, a letter whose dating eludes precision.

> Brother Leo, health and peace from Brother Francis! My son, I speak to you in this way – as a mother would – because I put everything we said on the road in this brief message and advice. Afterwards, if you need to come to me for counsel, I advise you thus: In whatever way it seems better to you to please the Lord God and to follow his footprints and poverty, do it with the blessing of the Lord God and my obedience. And if you need and want to come to me for the sake of your soul or for some consolation, Leo, come.

Facilitators need first of all to help participants to relax and take a brief look at the overall process in its three phases:

Humility; Sisterhood/Brotherhood; Peace. They begin by envisioning themselves as people who are truly beloved. This can be done by asking them to be still, to do nothing, to allow for the activity of God who loves them, desires their friendship and understands them with compassion. This will mean accepting that, even without doing anything, this God rejoices in their company and wants them to move to their true potentiality, greatness and destiny.

This process calls for accepting the possibility of being loved unconditionally, an experience that is not the lot of many people. Entering into solitude and silence will allow the participants to reflect on events and circumstances in their lives, past and present, so that they can leave themselves open to receiving what will be given.

It may be that none of the events in our lives approximates to those in the life of Francis, for example, his imprisonment. This experience may have brought home to him the many other ways in which he was imprisoned. Many people and events were distasteful to him but he discovered that what he disliked in others were the very traits and attitudes that he mirrored in himself. He was afraid of these and was not reconciled with them. Therefore, what he rejected in others, he was rejecting in himself. In rejecting what was in himself he was equally rejecting God, to whom the lovableness of each one of us is without question: 'You are my beloved one, in whom I am well pleased' (Mt 3:17). In Jesus we are now the beloved ones. Participants can be encouraged to come to terms with this, and to help each other to do so. In private contemplation also, their own lovableness before God must be embraced as reality. Acceptance of that which we find difficult to embrace in ourselves and in others, and the realisation that there is no part of us that is not lovable to God, is all part of the one process. Otherwise, there is a barrier to seeing creation as God sees it. God sees what is really there. 'And God looked at everything he had made, and he found it very good' (Gen 1:31).

It is often difficult for us to come to genuine awareness of our lovableness, and of how God loves us unconditionally. For that reason, it is worthwhile recalling participants to solitude, contemplation and remembrance, so that this revelation will take root and become a source of joy. The effects will lead into a cycle of contemplation, love, decision and action.

Participants need to develop the realisation that lovableness is constant with God, regardless of our actions or dispositions, whether good or bad. What is desired by God above all is our faith and trust. It is only in faith and trust that we will be able to love and to receive fullness of life.

For reading, the participants can look at the discussions and reflections in Part Three, and scriptural texts such as the Beatitudes, and realise that the 'poor in spirit' (Mt 5:1-11) are in right relationship with God and therefore with fellow human beings. The materially poor are also in right relationship with God because, in their need for help and acceptance, they automatically draw God's compassion and blessing. If, however, in their need, they are driven to undue bitterness and resentment, they can fail to enter into the blessings intended for them.

Any of the discussions or reflections in Part Three, even one quotation, can be given to the participants to stimulate reflection. We cannot put a time or limit to the working of God's mercy, love and grace. It can be pointed out to the participants that we are all enriched by helping one another in an understanding and appreciation of God as loving and merciful. That does not mean that there will not be times when we will feel as if we are alone. A programme such as this might be the very time for a sense of loneliness to be experienced.

Participants and facilitators will often find that one of the most difficult decisions is to accept that forgiveness and unconditional love are a free gift of God and not something earned. This is where God's love is so different from ours.

We can resist the experience of unconditional, gratuitous love and forgiveness. We want always to *earn* it. Reflection on this difficulty is necessary and deserves one or two sessions of reflective sharing. Discussing the possibility of refusing unconditional love and forgiveness, and how that might affect all our relationships, can be very helpful.

As we move into this acceptance, we become able to let go of previous stances and to do the truth in love. Then we will experience the freedom that the gospel promises, so that we will cease manipulating people and begin to live truthfully and lovingly in service of our fellow human beings.

PART ONE: INTRODUCTION TO FRANCISCAN SPIRITUALITY

In Part One we reflect on the human tendency to avoid reality by failing to hear and act on the truth that is in the heart of each one of us. We allow ourselves to be governed by our fears and illusions, consequently we fail to grasp all the blessings intended for us by the Creator. The follower of Jesus learns by the example of Jesus' life and death how to be free of falsity, and therefore to experience true peace and freedom.

Francis and Clare followed in the footsteps of Jesus and the testimony of their lives can be a beacon for us as it has been for many through the centuries. An account of each of their stories is given.

PART TWO: PROCESS/PROGRAMME FOR FRANCISCAN SPIRITUALITY

Part Two introduces us to the core of the spirituality of Francis and Clare. It is characterised essentially by three thrusts: by humility; by a family-type love of equality in sisterhood and brotherhood; and finally by peace.

Since *humility* anchors us in right relationship to God as beings created out of love, it follows that we are all equal in the sight of God, as *brothers and sisters* in the family of humanity. Appreciation of these two realities brings *peace*.

Phase I: Humility

We discover the 'me' whom God cherishes and desires. The kind of relationships I have and my response to them have helped make me who I am. Expectations, reactions, responses, decisions, my parents, my friends, my enemies, all of the people around me, are a part of who I am. All are involved, albeit unconsciously, in the response that I am now giving to life. Why do I do what I do? Why am I going where I am going? I may not be conscious of any directions. I may not know! This will be one of the main themes of the first phase, humility. Traditionally, the devil was called the father of lies, the master of illusion. We must ask the question: Who, really, am I?

We will enter into the life events of Francis and Clare as well as our own lives in order to appreciate that life's events can speak to us. In solitude we will reflect, allowing life events to speak to us in order to recognise their spiritual significance. These were the stages that Francis and Clare went through in their lives as they related to the God who revealed himself in Jesus Christ, who came that we might have abundant life.

From bitterness to sweetness, from death to life, from sin to wholeness: this is the journey, the discovery and the method. The Franciscan method can help us journey in a positive, uplifting direction if we, like Francis and Clare, accept the God who is on our side. This God can only give life. God's nature is to give life. God is also the Creator. As we see in the lives of Francis and Clare, the journey is always a process. For the first phase, on Humility, we need to grasp how beautiful and loving God is, in order to be able to comprehend that, for Francis, humility was an appreciation of all that is beautiful, and an understanding that the creature imaged the Creator. When he called his followers the lesser brothers *(minores),* he was not belittling them. He merely wanted to bring their true greatness into focus by mirroring to them the greatness of God. They were the beloved of God. Without God we are nothing. We did not create our own life, nor do we sustain ourselves in being. When human beings desire us to do their will, they try to enforce it, but the freedom God gives us is our opportunity to love. God always respects our freedom. Every one of God's creatures is uniquely beloved. This appreciation helps us discover our uniqueness in God and with God. The God of Jesus Christ loves each of us as if we were the only one.

Phase II: Sisterhood and Brotherhood
From that first understanding of who we are, we move to understand and appreciate one another. We look at the quality of sisterhood and brotherhood in our relationships. Just as God the Father said to Jesus, 'You are my beloved Son' (Mt 3:17; Mk 1:11; Lk 3:22), So He says to each of us, 'So be imitators of God as beloved children' (Eph 5:1). God has no favourites. Therefore, Francis saw that turning towards our neighbour, our fellow creatures – sisters and brothers, was to live as one family, equal as children of the one God, as God intended. This fraternal living is what we are called to.

Phase III: Peace
In the last phase we emphasise that all of us are bound up in the universe. To feel related to every part of this universe is to appreciate the reality of who we are. Every created thing is related to us in some way. Eventually we must decide whether

or not we want to accept our role in the universe as bearers of peace and reconciliation. On our journeys we need help to sense the creative energy of the universe and the source of energy that guides all of creation. We should try to see that all created things are part of us and we are part of them. Each has a unique role, called to guide creation to unity. We are called to be instruments of peace. In reconciling all things together in Christ, we are preparing for the glory and the joy to come in that unity in diversity. There we will understand our own uniqueness, realising how and who we are in relation to the author of creation and to creation itself, and our call to be united as equals in God through Jesus Christ. If we make this journey through reflection, solitude and listening, through action, prayer and work, we will discover a sense of unity, peace, harmony, belonging and diversity.

In order for people coming from different backgrounds to participate fully, we will explore how Francis and Clare understood what it means to be humble, to be a sister or brother, to be bearers of peace.

PART THREE: RESOURCES FOR FACILITATORS

Not all of the resources that have been included need to be used. Our choice should be very much under the guidance of the Spirit, and may depend on the time, place, moment and group. This applies to whatever exercise is used. In fact, it is advisable that participants volunteer their own ideas or activities.
During this process participants can be invited to:

1. Contemplate words that have meaning for them, underline these words and see them in terms of experiences, particularly their own.

2. Express voluntarily their expectations or fears of the process upon which they are about to embark.

3. Be still in order to allow space for the power and love of the creative forces within them to be expressed from their own life history. This will be assisted by leaving aside, as far as possible, all mundane thoughts and preoccupations. This is not to suggest becoming totally passive, but rather to transcend and to reflect in a detached manner.

4. Reflect on their own lives. Some events will crowd in, some might be dim; none is unimportant. Participants can write or recall their earliest memories, the ones that stand out, the ones that hurt, the ones of which they may be ashamed. Sometimes the failures may be foremost in people's minds and may well have an important spiritual significance. Thus it is important that participants recall those events without fear, without self-judgement as to how they responded to them. These reflections will be for group sharing.

The variety of resources included in this publication will hopefully find echoes in the lives and experiences of many and provide light and guidance. The lives of Francis and Clare can illuminate our own lives and provide a guide for us.

Francis of Assisi, in his desire to give full freedom of activity to the Spirit, always displayed sensitivity to each individual's quest. Human beings have a tendency to create divisions and obstacles, but this is not true of the Creator, who is at all times life-giving.

> Oh the depth of the riches and wisdom and knowledge of God! How unsearchable are his judgements and how inscrutable his ways. (Rom 11:33)

Francis of Assisi spent five periods of forty days in special prayer during the year, and both he and Clare of Assisi were convinced that *everything* of value must be performed 'above all else' with the Spirit of the Lord at work in our lives.[3] For that reason, there is absolute freedom of usage of this work – in whatever way it seems helpful, and to any group or individuals, or on any time scale as long as it is done with the Spirit of the Lord and His Holy operations.[4]

Shortly before the death of St Francis, he said to his brothers: 'I have done what is mine to do: May Christ teach you what is yours.'[5]

> The Lord granted me, Brother Francis, to begin to do penance in this way: While I was in sin, it seemed very bitter to me to see lepers. And the Lord himself led me among them and I had mercy upon them. And when I left them, that which seemed bitter to me was changed into sweetness of soul and body; and afterward I lingered a little and left the world.[6]

METHODOLOGY

The methodology is flexible and adaptable to every individual. Francis and Clare both offer a way that respects the uniqueness of every human being, a way that enables us to appreciate our relatedness to all created things.

In presenting this material it is necessary to go through a lived experience. All participants, especially facilitators, need to be instruments of peace. Thus, each time exercises are undertaken there ought to be a sense of calm, leaving way for the Creator to be present and active. The longing of each participant to be part of the love and friendship that is at the heart of creation needs to be appreciated by all. The programme emphasises connectedness with a God who never ceases to be creative, to renew; a Creator who only and always gives life. This gift of life can be frustrated through powers that bring death, such as jealousies, bitterness, rejection, refusal of friendship, fears, condemnations, pride, greed, avarice and ambition.

Being at peace with oneself, with others and with the universe will be helpful in order to facilitate a process that will make more space for God to become transparent now in the participants' lives.

FOR FACILITATORS AND PARTICIPANTS
It has been said of Francis that he believed that all were called to preach the gospel, and at times it would be necessary to use words![7] He himself preached the gospel by the life he led. For that reason, if participants can bring to the programme the qualities of Francis, particularly compassion, humility and patience, then the greater will be the possibility of experiencing the activity of a God who ever seeks to renew.

A variety of key concepts will be used according to the needs of the participants. The simple titles of the phases will be elaborated in order that their meaning may become alive and evident. The programme will include time spent in solitude, as well as in working and relating, according to individual strengths. In each segment, exercises are suggested and handouts will be made available from the resource section.

The intention of the programme is that its ethos will carry through into our own lives. We will look back on our own personal histories. Events in our lives that we might not like to remember can be the events that shape our lives creatively and positively. In seeking out their spiritual meaning, we are thereby meeting God, who is actually talking to us through the events of our lives.

Examples used in the programme include events in the lives of Francis and Clare that had a profound effect upon them. We will contemplate, as they did, experiences in Scripture and relate them to our own lives, and we will also contemplate our own experiences and try to find their echo in Sacred Scripture.

It is essential in embarking on this process that we accept that *life has a meaning, and that fundamentally life is with us,* not against us. 'I have come that they may have life and have it in abundance' (Jn 10:10). It was precisely Francis' understanding of life, of the God of compassion and love, that was the guiding-force and the source of his joy and his consequent love and zeal.

TIMETABLE

The programme is designed for any length of time best suited to the needs, both spiritual and material, of those participating. However, it would require not less than a weekend. The fact that the created world with all its inhabitants mirrored for Francis and Clare the activity of the Creator should enable even 'the busiest' to contemplate the eternal in the present moment.

The following is a suggested weekend timetable. This can be expanded or compressed according to a preferred schedule. The leader facilitates and participates rather than directs the experience. The atmosphere and method of communication should be that of dialogue (listening with or for) rather than debate (listening against) or discussion (listening to). Although the process needs to be digested, the following will help in giving a bird's-eye view of its content:

WEEKEND RETREAT

Friday Evening
Arrival, Welcome, Name Tags

6:00 p.m.   Supper/Dinner

7:00 p.m.	Introduction to Franciscan (Creation) Spirituality
7:30 p.m.	PHASE I: Humility

Presentation: Who Am I?
Allow for dialogue in a circle.
1. Illusion
2. Identity
3. 'You are my beloved' (Eph5:1)
4. Contemplation

8:30 p.m.	Dispersal of group for one hour of quiet reflection. Allow the presence of God to be active as I contemplate the historical events, happenings and circumstances of my own life. God was and is there – whether I love or not.
9:30 p.m.	Regroup Communication of life experiences

Saturday

8:30 a.m.	Breakfast
9:30 a.m.	PHASE II: Sisterhood and Brotherhood

Presentation: The Fear That Separates Us
1. Some events and circumstances in the lives of Francis and Clare on the road to conversion
2. Love is inclusive

10:00 a.m.	Dispersal of group.
	Reflection time, with handouts on leprosy, lepers in the Middle Ages.
	1. Who is the 'leper' in my life – who is obnoxious to me?
	2. Who is the leper in today's society?
	3. With whom do I need to be reconciled? Whom do I need to make part of my family/community?
11:00 a.m.	Coffee/Tea Break
11:30 a.m.	Regroup.
	Communication of life dialogue in group – faith-sharing mode, not discussion or debate.
	Helpful questions
	'My peace.' 'What do I dread most?' Please keep this ___ (person, event, happening) away from me Lord!'
1:00 p.m.	Lunch
	After lunch, rest, walk outside, contemplation time. Solitude, if desired, should be possible.
3:30 p.m.	Afternoon tea
4:00 p.m.	*Presentation: Eucharistic Love Unites Us*
	Clare/Poverty, Francis/Leper.
	Word made flesh. Conversion images.

4:30 p.m.   Break

4:45 p.m.   Faith-sharing

6:00 p.m.   Supper

7:00 p.m.   Eucharistic preparation

8:00 p.m.   Eucharistic celebration followed by
                 party/get-together

Sunday
9:00 a.m.   Breakfast

10:00 a.m.   PHASE III: Peace

                 Presentation: The Love That Unites Us
                 1. Peace and Reconciliation/Mission
                 2. Sharing

12:00 p.m.   Regroup
                 Service of Reconciliation

1:30 p.m.   Lunch
                 Departure

With Francis and Clare, let us proceed as they did in whatever way it seems best for us in our generation to please the Lord God and follow his footprints.

> Your salvation lay in conversion and tranquillity.
> Your strength in complete trust. (Is 30:15)

PART ONE

INTRODUCTION TO FRANCISCAN SPIRITUALITY

FRANCIS OF ASSISI

Francis was born about 1182. It was a time of upheaval in Italian society – the old feudal system was passing, new control centres or power bases were coming into being in the cities, and the people who held, or were about to hold, power were merchants. While nobility was declining in some respects, titles were still desired and could possibly now be bought by the new, emerging instrument of power – money. Pietro Bernardone, Francis' father, was a prominent member of the emerging merchant class, and money, clocks and schedules were a new phenomenon.

In such a climate, the future looked brighter for his favourite, charismatic son, John Pietro Bernardone. He may have had three sons – he certainly had two – the other being Angelo. However, John Pietro was the favourite. He even gave him a nickname – Francesco – after his beloved France, where he bought most of his merchandise and where he may have met his wife, Pica.

Both parents were extremely proud of their outgoing, charming son. All of his biographers agree that during his teens Francis loved fine dress, singing, gaming, feasting and partying. He was generous, and because of his knowledge of France he was culturally the leader among his friends. At the same time, however, he was known to patch his luxurious clothes with rags.

Between the ages of thirteen and twenty he learned his father's business and travelled with caravans to France and different parts of Italy. Though not from a noble family, he lived like a king's son. Pietro Bernardone began to buy and possess a lot of land in Assisi. Up until then, only the nobility had owned land.

When Francis was twenty there was a war between the

nobility and the communes in Assisi. Francis fought on behalf of the communes. The war escalated as the nobles fled to Perugia, and Perugia went to war with Assisi. Perugia won the war, and at twenty-one years of age Francis was taken prisoner for one year. Imprisonment affects people in different ways – some get depressed, some embittered, some vindictive. Francis became reflective. This was added to when he returned home and became seriously ill for a prolonged period of time. He was disappointed; as an ambitious young man he had hoped he might have been given a knighthood for his valour and bravery in war. He had the money to have the best of horses and armour, so in spite of his lack of blue-bloodedness, he would have had an opportunity to become a knight. Between the ages of twenty-two and twenty-three he decided to go on a 'crusade' to Apulia. Perhaps now a knighthood might be his. However, he returned home without going to war.

Francis was a realist. He was now reflecting deeply – he had the humility to accept who he was and what he could do. Of course there was the prospect of huge wealth; but would this not be an illusion – an illusory knighthood and respectability bought with money? Francis thought so. He wondered where his life was leading, what was its meaning.

More and more he became convinced that he was on the road to discovering the real meaning and source of life and happiness. The event that he focused on intensely, the event that he would have to get to know and discover, was the historical event of God becoming man. For Francis, no other event affected the entire universe and its meaning and calling more than this.

Francis believed that this entrance and presence of the creative power and strength of God must be discovered and acted upon if one was to make a contribution to the furtherance of life, creativity and productivity in the real sense. The authority of this God comes not in power, intimidation, manipulation, threat and fear, but in vulnerability, love and service. Francis abandoned his knightly ambitions and made an about-turn.

His father noticed the change in Francis and may have construed that Francis had lost his senses, or certainly gone wayward. When Francis began to give away his fine clothes and possessions, his father thought Francis had taken leave of his senses. Despite reproach and scorn, Francis followed the path he believed to be the right one. His father, in exasperation, seems to have wanted to sever connections with Francis and to retrieve the money that Francis had given away apparently so heedlessly. The conflict between them brought them before Bishop Guido. At that time, ecclesiastical authority and civil authority had their respective jurisdictions. It is hard to know if Pietro was making an attempt to disinherit Francis completely so that he would have nothing at all, and would be prevented from giving away anything else, or whether it was a question of Francis claiming that he now was, even though a layman, under Church authority, and as such any kind of legal conflict that would arise between himself and his father would have to go before the Church authority. Thomas of Celano, in his Life of Saint Francis (first book), describes in Chapter VI how Francis stripped himself before the Bishop of Assisi:

> 14. When the father saw that he could not recall him from the journey he had begun, he became obsessed with recovering the money. The man of God had desired to spend it on feeding the poor and on the buildings of that place. But the one who did not love money could not be deceived even by this appearance of good, and the one who was bound by an affection for it was not disturbed in any way by its loss. The greatest scorner of the things of earth

and the outstanding seeker of heavenly riches had thrown it into the dust on the windowsill. When the money was found, the rage of his angry father was dampened a little and his thirsty greed was quenched a bit by its discovery. Then he led the son to the bishop of the city to make him renounce into the bishop's hands all rights of inheritance and return everything that he had. Not only did he not refuse this, but he hastened joyfully and eagerly to do what was demanded.

15. When he was in front of the bishop, he neither delayed nor hesitated, but immediately took off and threw down all his clothes and returned them to his father. He did not even keep his trousers on, and he was completely stripped bare before everyone. The bishop, observing his frame of mind and admiring his fervour and determination, got up and, gathering him in his own arms, covered him with the mantle he was wearing. He clearly understood that this was prompted by God and he knew that the action of the man of God, which he had personally observed, contained a mystery. After this he became his helper. Cherishing and comforting him, he embraced him in the depths of charity.[1]

Again, in the Legend of the Three Companions:

19. ...When the authorities saw how enraged Peter was they sent a messenger to summon Francis. But he answered that, since by divine grace he had obtained freedom, he was the servant only of God and therefore no longer owed obedience to the civil authorities but was outside their jurisdiction. The city counsellors did not wish to force the issue, and answered Peter that as Francis had entered the service of almighty God he was no longer their subject.

Peter then realised that no satisfaction was to be had from the civil authorities, so he repeated his accusation before the Bishop of Assisi. The Bishop, a wise and prudent man, sent word to Francis that he must appear and answer his father's indictment; and he replied to the messenger: 'I will willingly appear before the Lord Bishop who is the father and lord of souls.'

He, therefore, went to the Bishop who received him gladly saying: 'Your father is highly incensed and greatly scandalised by your conduct. If therefore you wish to serve God, you must first of all return him his money, which indeed may have been dishonestly acquired. God would not wish you to use it for restoring the church through sin on the part of your father, whose anger will abate when he gets the money back. Trust in the Lord, my son, and act manfully, fearing nothing, for he will help you and provide you with all that is necessary for repairing the church.'

20. Thereupon the servant of God rose joyfully, comforted by the Bishop's words and holding out the money, he said: 'My Lord Bishop, not only will I gladly give back the money which is my father's but also my clothes.' Going into the Bishop's room he stripped himself of his garments and placing the money on them he stood naked before the Bishop, his father, and all present and said: 'Listen all of you and mark my words. Hitherto I have called Peter Bernardone my father; but because I am resolved to serve God I return to him the money on account of which he was so perturbed and also the clothes I wore which are his; and from now on I will say "Our Father who art in heaven," and not Father Peter Bernardone.' On that occasion it was seen that the servant of God wore a hair shirt under his coloured clothes.

His father rose up burning with grief and anger and he gathered up the garments and money and carried them home. Those present at this scene took the side of Francis because Peter had left him without any clothing, and moved with pity, they started to weep over him.[2]

Decisions taken by Francis were never merely cerebral. It was not just a mental detachment or a legal statement that separated him from his father. Francis never divided himself into compartments of convenience. He never tried to escape the pain of involvement – be it rejection or derision. Conversion for him would have to be a passion, a full-blooded transforming fire. He had to confront himself with his intense likes and dislikes. He had to acknowledge them.

As a young man, Francis must have prayed above all else that he would never be afflicted with what he dreaded most – leprosy. Lepers were condemned to living outside society and a burial service was held for anyone discovered to have leprosy. Yet he went to live and work with them! His decision was one of faith in Jesus Christ, who became one with creation in its vulnerability, its growing pains and its sufferings, and who placed within it the potential of sharing life with God on an equal plane in all its fullness, joy and happiness.

For Francis, the simple fact of existence meant that God already cared – the Source of Life was continuing to act in all this creation. To join with Christ meant an entry into a sisterhood/brotherhood with all of creation in newness of life – plant life, human life, animal life. He told his brothers when collecting firewood not to take all the branches off the tree – everything must be given the hope of resurrection.

At the age of thirty-one, he was joined by a young noblewoman, Clare (Chiara di Favarone), twelve years his junior, who, up until six or seven years previously, had belonged to the

Roman nobility, at that time viewed as the enemy. Now she wanted to take this radical step with Francis – to follow Christ. She gave up her dowry. She ran away by stealth and secrecy. She had her hair cut off by Francis, thereby completely renouncing her status, and became a servant-girl. Her family – particularly the menfolk – were angry and tried to rescue her. Francis helped her get protection in two Benedictine convents. Clare later returned to San Damiano, where Francis had restarted his monastery.

By the age of thirty-seven or thirty-eight, Francis had thousands of followers, and Clare had become known as a holy, wise and courageous woman.

While Francis' father may have accepted Francis now that he was acclaimed by so many, Francis could not be reconciled with him. Francis felt that his father did not understand what he himself really valued. While his father might have valued him now for his fame, Francis felt that this was a false value. Francis simply wanted to be a humble servant to God who was his Lord and master.

At the age of forty-one, Francis wanted to share with people the 'flavour' of the God-made-man as dramatised in the Gospels, the vulnerable God. So he asked that at Christmas in Greccio, a real-life enactment be made for him of the God-become-child, with father, mother, baby, animals, angels, straw: he wanted to behold a *needy* baby, to 'see with my own eyes the discomfort of his baby needs'.

In the last years of his life, between the ages of forty-three and forty-four, Francis was very ill. He had resigned as head of the order at the age of thirty-eight and had returned to work with the lepers again. Some medical scholars claim that Francis died from leprosy.

The second great drama of the Gospels that was dear to Francis was the Passion. At the age of forty-two, he did not need to get a cross, or have someone play the part of Christ. God provided something more than drama for him – his stigmata. He died praising God for all of creation, even those creatures and things that hurt him. While he was ill, in 1225, he wrote his wonderful Canticle of Creatures. His prayer joined with that of Jesus Christ in creatively calling all of creation to unite, to reconcile and to try to recognise the destiny guaranteed for it – new life and new growth, as equals through Christ in the ongoing, great creative process of God.

The writer G. K. Chesterton was of the view that an atom bomb in the hands of Francis of Assisi would be quite harmless. In fact, with the attitude and mind of Francis, our great creative discoveries would have developed a better and more just world over the 700 years since his death. The splitting of the atom, nuclear fission, development of rockets, space travel and electronic communications would not have emerged from our destructive tendencies of greed and manipulation; from our desire to conquer, to bully and to possess. There would not have been a Hiroshima, a Nagasaki, an Auschwitz or a Rwanda. We would not have seen genocide, racism/nationalism or religious fundamentalism leading to fear, hatred and oppression. Francis' way is an answer to the creative voice within each of us.

Doctor Pat McKeon, a psychiatrist at St Patrick's Hospital, Dublin, spoke about Ireland, its accelerating affluence and the splintering of family and community life: 'We are being overly influenced by, and not analysing critically, the value systems which are being presented to us; whether it is the way we run our health services or our economy'. I believe that the future of society depends on our capacity to think in terms of *inclusion* and *integration*. Only if we make the decision of Francis of Assisi and see Christ as the centre of that integration and inclusivity will we have, in any country, a peaceful, free and fulfilled people, who are ready to share God's bounty as equals in Christ.

After hearing *within himself* the voice of a friend, Francis arose without hesitation, and like *another Samson*, fortified by Divine Grace, he *broke* the *bonds* of the *fleeting* world.[3]

The *voice* of that *friend* speaks within us also, encouraging us to break the bonds of prejudice, envy, jealousy and greed and walk with Francis in the footsteps of Christ – creatively working with our Creator.

CLARE OF ASSISI

Clare of Assisi (Chiara di Favarone di Offreduccio) was the third of five children and the oldest daughter born to one of the noble families of that city. The family included seven knights. The year of Clare's birth is generally accepted as 1193. Most of the information about her life is found in the Acts of the Process of Canonisation, the testimony of those who knew her, recorded in November 1253. Caught in the difficulties of the time, resulting from the rise of the merchant class in Assisi, Clare's family fled to Perugia when she was still a child and returned to Assisi in 1205, when she was about twelve years old. That was the same year in which Francis of Assisi renounced his father and received official recognition by the Church of his life as a penitent. As an adolescent, Clare lived as a penitent also in her father's house. The Process tells us that her charity, generosity, compassion for the poor and dedication to prayer were well known even before her 'conversion' by Francis. Ortulana, Clare's mother, was a devout woman who had made a number of religious pilgrimages.

At that time marriages were often made at the age of twelve – and property, prosperity, nobility and beauty counted. Clare was a very beautiful woman. This evidence was given in the Process of her Canonisation. Therefore, she would not have been short of suitors. Clare obviously made a conscious decision not to marry and it is quite evident that from an early age she decided to answer a call much deeper in her own heart. Much later, in a letter to another noblewoman who had been engaged to the emperor Frederic II, she was to write: 'what a great and praiseworthy exchange: to leave the things of time for those of eternity, to choose the things of heaven for the goods of earth, to receive the hundred-fold in place of one, and to possess a blessed eternal life!'[1]

Apparently she heard Francis speak on one occasion and his radical decision to reverse completely his way of life and values struck a cord deep within her. On Palm Sunday 1212, when she was eighteen years of age, she decided to act. She left her home by a side door with the help of servants, and made for the little church of St Mary of the Angels, where Francis and the brothers were waiting. She put aside all her jewellery and had her beautiful long hair cut. Like Francis, she had discovered the God who for love of every human being had become 'contemptible and vulnerable'. This God had entered a transient world, a world different from the God-world, in order to be her friend, lover, servant, confidante. 'If so great and good a Lord, then, on coming into the virgin's womb, chose to appear despised, needy and poor in this world [cf. 2 Cor 8:9], so that people who are in utter poverty, want and absolute need of heavenly nourishment might become rich in Him by possessing the kingdom of heaven, be very joyful and glad! [cf. Heb 3:18]. Be filled with a remarkable happiness and a spiritual joy'.[2] For Clare, God the Father first impoverished himself, and the Lord Jesus embraced poverty before all else: 'The word became flesh so that flesh might become the word'.

In a class-conscious society, Clare had really embraced the 'leper' by rejecting the social values of her background and joining Francis. After a short stay as a servant in two Benedictine convents, Clare moved to San Damiano, the church that Francis himself had physically rebuilt. It was within this monastery that she lived with her sisters, the Poor Clares, for forty-one years, until her death in 1253. One of the sisters, on being questioned during the Process of Canonisation regarding the source of Lady Clare's holiness, replied, 'most especially in her love of the privilege of poverty'.[3]

This poverty of littleness, service and humility would be what distinguished the sisters. Francis said to the sisters: 'Those who are weighed down by sickness, and the others who are wearied because of them, all of you, bear it in peace, for you will sell this fatigue at a very high price'. In her Fourth Letter to Agnes of Prague she exclaims, 'Oh marvellous humility, oh astonishing poverty.'[4]

Pope Gregory tried to dissuade her from this path, suspecting that it might be the Franciscans who were encouraging her to take such a strong, radical way. He decided to prevent the Franciscans from influencing the Poor Clares and from being their spiritual directors. Clare went on hunger strike. Gregory IX did not want a starving community and, since the Franciscans protested on their behalf, he relented.

The fact that both Clare and Francis left home and turned their backs on their families, constituted a scandal. However, for both of them it was the same type of scandal, of 'self-emptying', as 'the word becoming flesh'. Pietro de Damiano, a next-door neighbour of Clare, said that Clare's parents wanted Clare to marry someone great and powerful, in keeping with her nobility. However, even before following Francis, she was heading for a different way of life, as she had sold all her inheritance and given it to the poor.[5] The fact that their families were so much against their choices shows that, as individuals, Francis and Clare were prepared to take big risks and launch into the deep in order to discover the real meaning of life. At the end of her life, Clare's words were: 'Go, securely and in peace, for you have a good escort for your journey; go for he who created you made you holy'.

PRELIMINARIES FOR UNDERSTANDING FRANCISCAN (CREATION) SPIRITUALITY

Fear of Reality – Who am I?

We tend to be afraid of reality and to delight in using illusions and fantasies for recreational purposes. We sometimes come to believe these to be reality. However, our avoidance and fearfulness of reality, especially when it contradicts our false opinions and inspirations, are things that we need to address when we start to pay attention to our fundamental yearnings and their ultimate fulfilment.

The journey to the core of our being to discover the hidden treasure there, is one that we can find very difficult to make. This is because we run away from our self, our real self, believing it to be somehow unacceptable. Often our dreams are built on anything but self-acceptance. In this non-acceptance of the real self, we are also meeting other people in a similar state of fear, and we feel threatened. Instead of building for life to give life, we build fences and place walls around ourselves so that we are in conflict with other people. 'This world' becomes reality for us. We are often afraid to tell others who we are, to tell God who we are, even to tell ourselves who we are. We tend to build our world around ourselves. Because of their faith and trust, Francis and Clare arrived at great self-knowledge. 'It is absurd to think we can enter Heaven without first entering our own souls, without getting to know ourselves....'[1]

Shattering our Illusions

We surround ourselves with all kinds of insulation to cover the 'self' in the heart. Francis' fear that his 'self' would become leprous made the leper repulsive to him. He surrounded his 'self' early on with fine clothing, a desire for knighthood and a respectable reputation. However, events began to shatter some of his aspirations, and he realised that only the journey to his authentic 'self' would uncover what God had created. When he turned aside from his usual preoccupations and paid attention to what really mattered, he found what he had not anticipated, that not only could he accept what had previously been hateful to him, but he could embrace it with joy. This applied to everything, not just lepers. Bitterness was transformed into sweetness. Joy pervaded everything.

Francis' decision to divest himself of everything to the point of nakedness brought him rapidly into the heart of reality. He discovered God and thereby himself. The Creator is light and life. It is in our darkness and death that the Creator suddenly illuminates everything with new life and light.

Call to Destiny

You and I have been created so that we can inherit the life, power, generosity, love and creativity of God. All of creation is an act of generosity. As beings with freedom, we often do not appreciate that we are *created*, and, though we are God's creatures, we desire to 'play God'. In misuse of our freedom, we often lose sight of our origins and of the fact that everything was given to us as gift. This results in the living of lives based on fear, with secret greed among ourselves leading to divisions, laying of blame, selfishness and guilt, instead of gratitude and the desire to share, to respect and to give life.

Anthony de Mello likens us to eagles reared by chickens, learning only chicken language until our nature is stirred by the presence of eagles flying overhead, as we realise that we have a different destiny. Christ came into the world as a human being so that we might return to God as equals in Christ, once Christ had shown us the way. We are often a poor image of our Creator because of our inability to see or respond to the generosity that has been showered upon us. There are, nevertheless, many human beings who have discovered 'the pearl of great value' (cf. Mt 13:46) and who perceive what God set out to do in Christ.

God gave his only Son as a gift, who suffered for us and shared our joys and sorrows. We are invited to join in a relationship of life and love as equals in Jesus Christ. Through the energy (spirit) of the Risen Jesus, our lives can become imbued with creativity, hope and joy, no matter what our circumstances are (cf. Eph 4:1-6).

'Yes' to the Invitation of the Creator
The chief reality in which we are immersed is creation in all its wonder and bounty. To say 'yes' to the invitation of the Creator is a 'yes' to reality – not to illusion. Each moment is a moment that calls for trust. As we look back on our history, there are many decisions and events in our lives from which we can learn. It is precisely at the times of the unfolding of these events, and the consequent decisions that we make, that we are choosing either to live a life based on reality, or one that evades reality. The Creator calls each of us by name and has a purpose and mission for each of us. Discovering the part that we are invited to play, and acting on it, is the 'pearl of great price' – the treasure.

Rediscovery and Acceptance of Self
The Creator God can only give life – there is nothing destructive in God. We have guides such as Francis and Clare who took the Incarnation very seriously, the word becoming flesh so that the flesh would become word (cf. Jn 1:14.12). In doing this they left status and achievements aside and elected to have only one privilege, that of not being privileged. This was the reality they grasped about Jesus Christ, who left aside all privileges. This is the secret wisdom, the going to a 'lower place' (cf. Phil 2:7), and thereby discovering who we are, and the

acceptance of who we are with joy. This is the secret strength of letting go, and thereby becoming instruments of peace and joy. If we begin to mirror God's action we automatically promote justice, peace, integrity and hope. 'What a man is before God, that he is and no more.'[2] Francis and Clare and the other saints reassure us that what the Creator achieved in them can be achieved in our age through us as well.

To be a peaceful person and to be able to reflect the compassion of the Creator to others, we need to be in touch with our creaturehood, our own humanness, our total dependence on the Creator, and to be able to be compassionate towards ourselves. We need to begin to discern the presence of the Creator in our experience – in the circumstances and events of our lives. Our relationship with one another in sisterhood and brotherhood needs to be one of mutual acceptance and affirmation. We need to be conscious of our responsibility to reach out, especially to the vulnerable, with the utmost compassion. Only in this way can we become instruments of peace in our age.

> It was as if I suddenly saw the secret beauty of their hearts, the depths of their hearts where neither sin, nor desire, nor self-knowledge can reach, the core of their reality, the person each one is in God's eyes. If only they could all see themselves, as they really are. If only we could see each other that way all the time. There would be no more war, no more hatred, no more cruelty, and no more greed.[3]

Opening the Heart to Prayer

Prayer, which is opening the heart to the Creator and being totally honest with the Creator, weans us away from our normal tendency to illusion. Instead of taking the way of trust, we are usually more preoccupied with building a monument of achievements. In contrast, friendship with the Creator results in an emphasis on fruitfulness and not on our personal achievements. Fruitfulness implies preparation, readiness, openness and receptivity. It is a different kind of work to that of achievement, which implies striving and competition. Contact with the Creator through prayer, therefore, helps us to get to know the Creator ever more intimately. It is in this light that we come to know ourselves, to know the part we have to play in conjunction with others in saying 'yes' to the Creator's invitation, which is the building up of the harmony, unity and the interdependence of all of creation. In stressing fruitfulness rather than achievement, and in following the way of Jesus Christ as the way of being truly human and fulfilled, we cherish each moment as an opportunity.

> The heart is to be understood here, not in its ordinary meaning, but in the sense of 'inner person'. We have within us an inner person, according to the Apostle Paul, or a hidden person of the heart, according to the Apostle Peter. It is the God-like spirit that was breathed into the first man, and it remains with us continuously, even after the fall.[4]

Yielding to the Healing of the Spirit

The divine will is expressed in every aspect of reality. The Good News invites us to be fruitful. The ethos of our society asks us to be achievers. The decisions and choices we make determine whether we are prepared to allow the Creator create with us and through us. If they are not aligned with the divine will, then we are trying to control our own sources of discernment; in effect, 'to be like God'. To live that lie is to reap an illusion.

Francis and Clare discerned that at the back of this lie was pride – refusing to accept the limitations of our creaturehood, appropriating to ourselves what is not ours. The motivation then, in that instance, is the desire to control. Jesus resisted the temptation to be in control, yielding his mind and heart to the Father's will so that we could join our state with his in trusting and abandoning ourselves to the Father. He chose freely to love and accept a trustworthy father, and to be loved by God, who loves unconditionally.

St Francis de Sales in his *Treatise on the Love of God* says, 'We are the image of one another, all of us representing only the one portrait who is God.'[5]

Jesus prays to the Father (Jn 17) that we be united together as he and the Father are united. Groups, with their variety of gifts, who, under the guidance of the Spirit, elect to journey creatively through this process, will experience that unity also. Thus, what at first seems beset with difficulties, yields to the outpouring and healing of the Spirit.

To acknowledge our limitations can be painful because it involves dismantling our defences and accepting others as the Creator does, with compassion. For Francis, to abandon everything was the beginning of a life-long journey. 'Now that we have left everything, all that need occupy us is to do the will of the Lord and please him alone.'[6]

God's Transforming Action

Both Francis and Clare saw that God signalled poverty and letting go as the key of love and friendship by giving what was most precious to him, the Son, so that all might live under blessings. Francis was prepared to let go of all that shielded him from what was repulsive to him – leprosy and the leper. He gave up status, inheritance and riches to become one of the leper brotherhood.[7] Clare also gave up her status and inheritance, and allowed her hair to be cut off in order to become one with those who had no privilege.

Francis discerned that poverty of spirit was enriching beyond measure; that becoming vulnerable clothed him in strength – not his own but that of the Creator. He had discovered the biblical 'pearl of great price'. Those who choose this way become enriched and strengthened in the only ways that ultimately matter.

Letting Go

We often pursue the wrong path sincerely but blindly. We are like a person with a broken ankle who wrongly exercises it in order to heal it and take away the pain. The desert fathers of old were aware of this tendency to react with a wrong solution; they pointed out the need for us to go the other way.

> It was said of the Abba John that, having gone off to Scete to an old man of Thebes, he remained in the desert. His Abba took a dry stick and planted it and told him: 'Water this every day with a flask of water until it bears fruit.' But the water was so far away that he would leave in the evening and return in the morning. After three years, though, it came to life and bore fruit. And the old man took the fruit, carried it to the church and said to the brethren: 'Take and eat the fruit of obedience'.[8]

Obedience, when it is a suffering, can be part of one's training, as the letter to the Hebrews indicates (cf. Heb 12:11). In God's providence, no one is meant to be barren. Isaiah stresses that with God, everyone can bear fruit. Everyone is called to bring life.

> Sing. O barren one who did not bear! Break forth into singing and cry aloud you who have been in travail! For the children of the desolate one will be more than the children of her that is married, says the Lord. (Is 54:1-2)

It is in the process of letting go rather than 'clinging/possessing', that we can become 'poor' in the *biblical* sense (cf. Lk 6:20-22). Henri Nouwen was very impressed with the example of a circus family (the Flying Rodleighs) who performed on the trapeze. In a dangerous trapeze act, one of the artists would take a jump into the air blindfolded. The important person, however, is the catcher. The person who makes the dramatic jump must do it at a certain time, being totally relaxed and full of trust, in such a way that all is left in the hands of the catcher – the arms and hands are stretched out and the rest is trust. Any form of panic or loss of trust can result in the death of either, or, at best, in broken wrists. Jesus is the example of this trust in the Father as he makes his life journey, letting go in trust that the Father will grasp him ultimately. We, who are brought into existence by the Father, follow the way Jesus has trodden for us, which brings us, eventually, to the Father under the guidance of the Spirit. This is the path to unity, peace and harmony.

All our inner journeys involve farewells that are a letting go in prayer and trust. We say goodbye to seeming safety and security and we risk setting out on paths that take us through ways of decay, pain and vulnerability. This is the narrow passage into the way of life and ultimately to our true fulfilment, which is God's intention for us (cf. Mt 7:13, Lk 13:24).

Solitude
Journeying in solitude can be another aspect of suffering that ultimately leads to fulfilment. If we cannot be alone with ourselves and be at peace in our own company, how can we expect others to appreciate our companionship? The danger is that we fill ourselves with fantasies in order to drug the fear and pain of apparent loneliness instead of allowing ourselves to be led to the depths of our hearts. Solitude helps us come to terms with our own needs. The desert fathers by their lives as solitaries

give us a concrete example of what it means to turn aside from everything in order to attain true self-knowledge. When we allow our loneliness to become deep solitude, we create space where we can begin to hear the voice that calls each of us individually. All the experiences of loneliness, sickness, suffering and death can be opportunities for trust in and dependence on the Creator, who through these negative experiences confers life. Within the Creator's intention and design, our loneliness is meant to and can become fruitful.

The Pearl of Great Value

The Bright Field

I have seen the sun break through
To illuminate a small field
For a while, and gone my way
And forgotten it. But that was the pearl
Of great price, the one field that had
The treasure in it. I realise now
That I must give all that I have
To possess it. Life is not hurrying

On to a receding future nor hankering after
An imagined past. It is the turning
Aside like Moses to the miracle
Of the lit bush, to a brightness
That seemed as transitory as your youth
Once, but is the eternity that awaits you.
(R. S. Thomas)[9]

At the core of who we are there is a sacred treasure, and the Creator holds the key to our individual destinies. We exist because of love and we are born for love. For that reason we are endowed with freedom and choice.

Solitude helps us to shed the false adherence and camouflage of years. The true self can function with the help of the Creator. This is what Francis and Clare came to experience. We need the faith and courage to realise that the end of our journey into reality is the finding of our true selves. This is the pearl of great value, and on finding it we come to the source of Joy. Not infrequently, testing life events accelerate the process of uncovering reality and force us to make the journey that we might not otherwise have undertaken.

> And every human heart that breaks,
> In prison-cell or yard,
> Is as that broken box that gave
> Its treasure to the Lord,
> And filled the unclean leper's house
> With the scent of costliest nard.
> Ah! Happy they whose hearts can break
> And peace and pardon win!
> How else may man make straight his plan
> And cleanse his soul from Sin?
> How else but through a broken heart
> May Lord Christ enter in?
> (Oscar Wilde)[10]

Doing the Truth in Love

When groups of people come together to renew themselves they will require radical honesty and openness, such as that manifested by Francis and Clare when they responded, in their time, as followers of Christ. Both decided in a very radical way to leave status, wealth and achievement behind in order to become the least. The unsought outcome of this was that they had a tremendous influence on their generation, so that even to this day they provide a sound guide to people who would embark on this road now. This process allows sufficient creativity and flexibility for any group or person to be open to the Spirit in their own way.

We are beckoned by Christ to become vulnerable as he became vulnerable, doing the truth in love. A group embarking on this process needs the ability to enter into periods of quietness to allow the creative power within them to come to the surface. We can be blinkered by obstacles such as ambition, envy or jealousy, and so impede the work of the Spirit in us. To desire genuinely to have listening hearts is a requisite for all who would ultimately derive fruit from this process.

Conclusion

We human beings tend to act egotistically. Christ has shown us another way which opens us to the Father. The spirit of truth dwelling in us is the treasure that lies hidden behind the façade constructed by us, and by society, which prevents us facing up to ourselves. If we remove our masks and abandon our subterfuges, then the Spirit within us will be released and we will be transformed by its power into a new way of thinking and being. We will acknowledge that God is at the centre of all that is, and not ourselves. We will experience the freedom of being loved unconditionally in our uniqueness. There will be no need to justify ourselves. Our conscience will make us painfully aware of how we have not acknowledged and responded to the Spirit of Truth in the past – to 'the law written in people's hearts' (Rom 2: 14-15). Conscience will also make us aware of the degree of desire and willingness to respond at present and in the future. If we remain open to the promptings of the Spirit and submit to the purification of our consciousness, we will be in communication with God at the deepest level, that of the heart.

> Let us begin, brothers, to serve the Lord God for up until now we have done little or nothing.[11]

PART TWO

PROCESS/PROGRAMME FOR FRANCISCAN SPIRITUALITY

PHASE I – HUMILITY

> Humility is a stance of realistic, unashamed acceptance of my finitude... both what I can do and what I cannot do... in relation to God, the cosmic limiter. Also the cosmic enabler and encourager.[1]

> When he is drawn to think about his real self he turns to those deep recesses of his being where God who probes the heart awaits him, and where he himself decides his own destiny in the sight of God.[2]

As we begin our journey to discover the joy that Francis discovered, we consider the delight that he experienced in humility, calling himself and his brothers 'the lesser brothers'. For someone who had high aspirations and every likelihood of achieving many of them through his position in the merchant class, this was not a grovelling acceptance of himself as a non-entity. Rather, it was an understanding that real power and beauty reside in the activity of the Creator. Our beauty is but a reflection of the Creator. To be lesser, then, is to be in right relationship with the Creator and therefore to experience life in abundance. To be lesser is to acknowledge being a useless servant, who is elevated to greatness through God's power.

The dreams we have of our own making will at some stage, even though it may take years, eventually show themselves to be without solid substance. Life has a habit of throwing darts at our balloons.

All of us live in illusion, at least at times. Some of the events in Francis' life broke the illusions he had, and this opened a new reality to him.

Francis reflected on the events of the life of Jesus Christ as described in the Gospels and entered them as an actor might enter a drama. In doing so, he saw their spiritual significance. If we enter into the drama and reflect on the birth of Jesus, we also may experience the vulnerability of nakedness, with no room at the inn, the depiction of a strange place, the protection of shepherds, the company of the animals. We find just two people and their child, strangers away from home (Lk 2:1-20; Mt 2:1-15). The birth story emphasises neither power nor glory, but vulnerability, nakedness and insecurity. It gave to Francis a sense of the way God enters our lives and history. The story is not surrounded by the 'spectacular'. Mary pondered all these events in her heart, and we should ponder all the events of our lives, too, because they will speak to us if we listen. The present moment is always precious, and now is the time when our life events can surface in a very meaningful way.

Since the time of Francis, many have entered deeply into the mystery of God. To do this with others is enriching, as it enlivens and facilitates the process. Francis did not proceed alone; he was joined by Peter Catanii, a priest, by Bernard of Quintavalle, a wealthy layman, and of course by Clare. She consented to set out on a unique road. It was the Lord who took the initiative in her life as he took it in Francis'. She would say: '… the most heavenly Father saw fit in His mercy and grace, to enlighten my heart.'[3] Life was a gift and God enlightened her heart that she should acknowledge that gift by a total turning to the Giver. It was a turning away from her family, from the so-called 'real' world, from proposals of marriage of distinction, and a turning instead towards those who would be considered the insignificant poor, and seeing them as if for the first time.

> He took the blind man by the hand and led him outside the village. Then, putting spittle on his eyes and laying his hands on him, he asked, 'Can you see anything?' The man,

who was beginning to see, replied, 'I can see people; they look like trees to me, but they are walking about.' Then he laid his hands on the man's eyes again, and he saw clearly. He was cured, and he could see everything plainly and distinctly. (Mk 8:22-26)

For Francis, his new journey was one in which the events of his own life became ever deeper in significance as they disclosed to him the power of a God who was in love with every minute detail of his creation, and who knew each individual intimately. An event that had a profound effect on Francis was his one-year imprisonment. Such an event in any of our lives would take its toll. The outcome need not be negative; it could be positive.

The conversion of St Paul is possibly one of the most dramatic accounts of conversion. The following is a dialogue between Malcolm Muggeridge and Alec Vidler, where they talk about Paul's conversion and his need for a quiet place or solitude, as most people do who have had a 'shattering experience'.

ALEC
In one of his letters Paul describes how after his conversion he went off on his own so as to be able to reckon with the consequences of what had happened to him.

…when he who had set me apart before I was born, and had called me through his grace, was pleased to reveal his Son to me, in order that I might preach him among the Gentiles, I did not confer with flesh and blood, nor did I go up to Jerusalem to those who were apostles before me, but I went away into Arabia (Gal 1:15-17).

Arabia, that means the desert. Even today, anybody who has had a shattering experience wants to get away somewhere to sort it out in quietness and solitude. And in the Bible nearly everyone who had a great experience did this – Moses, Elijah, John the Baptist; Jesus after his baptism went into the desert. It is natural that Paul should do the same. Practically all his earlier beliefs had been turned inside out. For instance, until now he'd thought of Jesus as a dead pretender, but now he was absolutely convinced that he was the living Lord, the centre of a new creation, a new world, which was going to make everything different for him.

MALCOLM
I was going to ask you about that, because he's always talking about being 'in Christ'.

ALEC
Yes, he uses the expression again and again. It means, I would say, that Christ was, as it were, the new atmosphere in which he was going to live and breathe and which he was always going to depend upon. And he wanted everyone else to live in this atmosphere and to breathe it.

Then again, the cross was absolutely different for him now. Up till now the idea of a crucified Messiah had been an intolerable scandal, but now he was convinced that on the cross the Son of God had given himself for him and had saved him from the frustration in which he'd been trying to put himself right with God through doing the works of the Law and by earning merit. What he saw now was that God had taken the initiative in Christ and with amazing generosity had accepted him as an adopted son, just as he was, despite his abject unworthiness, and without his having to sweat away to get right with God by his own self-centred efforts. He had only to put his whole trust in what God had done for him in Christ and then to live out his life in thankfulness for that.[4]

All crises demand decisions and choices in our lives. 'Man has both potentialities within himself; which one is actualised depends upon decisions but not upon conditions.'[5]

> Only a moment's reflection on those significant occasions in our own lives when we felt that we had enlarged the boundaries of our selfhood and experienced a deeper sense of self-worth, will reveal that these were rare and special times when we took charge of our lives, made a decision out of our own strength and moved toward a goal which we found both attractive and compelling. We acted out of our own strength from no other compulsion except our inner desire to achieve an envisioned good. It is these self-decisions which are the sure point of human growth and movement and our creative decision blossoms best only when freed from all external constraint. In sum, we are persons and not objects, and we are most true to our essential selfhood when we respond from the wealth of our own power of choice, rather than when power is imposed upon us.[6]

'Now I understand that to be filled with wisdom, one must first, through suffering, be emptied of illusions and false dependencies.' So said Duane Beane, who served one year in prison for his part in the Missouri Peace Planting in 1989. His one-year imprisonment enabled him to give us the following insights:

Gradually, however, I discovered the things that most aggravated me about others' behaviour, were the same traits I was not ashamed of in myself – selfishness, insensitivity, pettiness, intolerance. My antipathy towards others was, in fact, a projection of my own inner brokenness. To simply be, instead of being obsessed with doing, continues to be my toughest test. One need not be a hero in prison; being fully human is enough.[7]

God, as imaged in the Hebrew Bible, seeks an unfaithful people with the longing of a rejected lover (Hos 2) and remembers the people with a mother's love (Is 49:14-15). In our decision to leave space for God's activity, we need to allow God to be God, to give the benefit of the doubt to God, and to leave ourselves open to the longing of One who loves us as no one else can. Perhaps it is only in poverty of spirit that we can allow this to happen.

For many people, contemplation/prayer 'is a cry of recognition and of love, embracing both trial and joy' (Saint Therese of Lisieux). It is a question of our thirst for life being directed towards the thirst of God.[8] We discover how to centre ourselves by withdrawing. 'The heart is the place, again, to which I withdraw.'[9]

The heart is our hidden centre, beyond the grasp of our reason and of others; only the Spirit of God can fathom the human heart and know it fully. The heart is the place of decision, deeper than our psychic drives. It is the place of truth, where we choose life or death. It is the place of encounter, because as image of God we live in relation; it is the place of covenant.[10]

We can understand the God who listens to a prayer of humility as we kneel at the back of the church. We believe this is the way to pray, and we ourselves choose that way, but in reality we are praying the Pharisee's prayer, because in our hearts we say, 'Thank God, I'm not like the Pharisee.' It is very difficult to have hearts of humility, ready to receive, because it means *letting go of so much that is part of us*. Most of us have been taught always to defend ourselves and therefore we enclose our hearts and our vulnerability. Francis and Clare regarded even properties and possessions as defences. Francis said they only put us in conflict with others. Indeed, to expose our hearts to God or to anybody makes us very vulnerable. It is a decision to divest ourselves of all masks, to risk having to change, to become one who receives rather than gives, to become nothing and to have nothing to give in return. Most of us have never been in that position because we have retained some defensiveness, which is part and parcel of our conditioning and education. 'It's mine' is much more readily on the mouth of a child than 'it's yours', albeit that it denotes a stage of the child's development. G. K. Chesterton may be accurate when he says that we are not humble, nor do we understand what Francis meant by being lesser, because it is so foreign to us. Yet our happiness depends on this choice to be poor, to be 'lesser' in the example of the poor Christ.

> We cannot follow Saint Francis to that final spiritual overturn, in which complete humiliation becomes complete holiness or happiness, *because we have never been there.*[11]

To accept the necessity of diminishment and sorrow for our failures to love involves beginning again constantly. Even for Francis, there was always a returning to the initial step.

> Therefore, all my brothers, let us be very much on our guard, so that we do not lose or turn away our mind and

heart from the Lord under the guise of achieving some reward, or doing some work, or providing some help.[12]

When we read the Gospels we all tend to identify with whoever did the 'right' thing in a given situation, such as those outlined in Jesus' parables, and more particularly in the passion accounts, when we feel that we would not have deserted Jesus as his disciples did. We can see ourselves in the parable of the Pharisee and the tax-collector, and we may tend to identify with the prayer of the humble tax-collector.

In the parable of the two debtors (Lk 7:41-43) we can see our inability to accept the lovableness of every human being. Thus, in the mirror of the parable, we are meant to realise that we have not experienced our own lovableness, confirmed in the mercy of the Father in our lives. Accepting all that we are, both the positive and the negative, is to accept reality. This is a prerequisite for prayer; without such self-acceptance, our prayer is very immature.

Henri Nouwen, writing about the Father in the parable of the prodigal son, and the way Rembrandt has depicted the Father in his painting, says,

> As long as the Father evokes fear, he remains an outsider and cannot dwell within me. But Rembrandt, who showed me the Father in utmost vulnerability, made me come to the awareness that my final vocation is indeed to become like the Father and to live out his divine compassion in my daily life. Though I am both the younger son and the elder son, I am not to remain them, but to become the Father. No father or mother ever became father or mother without having been son or daughter, but every son and daughter has to consciously choose to step beyond their childhood and become father and mother for others. It is a hard and

lonely step to take, especially in this period of history in which parenthood is so hard to live well – but it is a step that is essential for the fulfilment of the spiritual journey.[13]

Francis' decision to cease 'doing', to stop striving for material benefits, and to experience forgiveness, love and acceptance, even during sickness or imprisonment, enabled him to say that the Lord had spoken to him. In his Testament at the end of his life we find such statements as 'The Lord granted me', 'the Lord himself led me,' 'the Lord gave me such faith', 'the Lord gave me brothers', 'the Lord revealed to me a greeting', and 'the Lord has granted me to speak and to write the Rule in these words simply and purely'.[14]

Because Francis could take that particular turn, and sought a different path, as Chesterton points out, he could say with great certainty that this Lord spoke to him. It was a sign of great wonder to him that the majesty of God could be broken down in the breaking of the bread for us. Jesus was the human face of God. 'Jesus is a lover; this is his secret, which can hardly be proclaimed, for it cannot be known outside an experience.'[15]

It is through the action and mercy of God's love for us that we are empowered to become loving people also. Otherwise, we attempt to use resources within ourselves somewhat as possessions, to buy love, to possess love. It is good for people to realise how subtly self-centred *our* loving is. It is liberating for us to come to an awareness of how conditional our loving can be. Often we fail to see that love is possible only if it comes from the source that is love, the Creator God.

> Let love be sincere; hate what is evil; hold on to what is good, love one another with mutual affection, anticipate one another in showing honour. (Rom 12:9-10)

Unlimited and unconditional love desires to give and share completely. It does not condemn. It takes the last place. That is the story of creation. The voice within us that tells us we are bad, that accuses us, is the voice of sin. When we justify ourselves, we are condemning one another because we ignore our relationship with the Creator. To receive the gift of life, as one who is beloved and good in the eyes of the Creator, is to live free of guilt and shame. The gift of creation urges us to gratitude and to be givers of life, not destroyers of it. Francis would say, '…return everything to the most high Lord God to Whom every good belongs'.[16]

Francis never ceases to be relevant. He was a simple, fairly uneducated person who centred his life in love and truth and thereby affected the lives of countless people for their good, from the Pope and his cardinals to Francis' own peers, and the outcasts, the lepers.

By the end of his life, his choice of being 'lesser' had propelled him to unsought fame and veneration. His Canticle of the Sun is an expression of the glory and the joy that were his.

PHASE II – SISTERHOOD AND BROTHERHOOD

Maybe when we reject people we are saying something about our own brokenness, our own incapacity to love, and maybe we will be healed by 'those we reject'.[1]

Relationships must not be hierarchical, from the unequal distribution of power, but absolutely fraternal, everyone being brothers and sisters, even where there are different functions, as it says in the Regula non-Bullata: Brothers who preach, pray, work, clerics and lay; that there be no prior, but rather ministers and servants. This fraternity which gives shape to the Church, must be open to all without distinction, even 'to thief or robber, to friend or adversary'.[2]

As noted in Phase I, Humility, we are concerned with God's agenda, not ours. We can recall how Jesus was concerned with God's agenda also:

Someone told him, 'Your mother and your brothers are standing outside, asking to speak with you'.... And stretching out his hand towards his disciples, he said, 'Here are my mother and my brothers. For whoever does the will of my heavenly Father is my brother, and sister, and mother.' (Mt 12:47, 49, 50)

The realisation of the activity of God in our lives may not be as acceptable to us as we might assume it to be. We have so much confidence in our own way of doing things that we generally rush ahead and rarely seek to discern God's will, or wait on God's presence in our actions. Even if we were told that God would come in the next hour, we would prepare things our way. The fact is, God is active now in our lives and we are ignoring that activity. In this section we look at the way we can allow God's activity to be part of our lives so that we can be transformed and can appreciate the way of life that asks us to let go of our own agenda.

A chart showing where we have arrived, how we have arrived, and where we are going can be very helpful for us. In the same way, consciousness of the path of Francis will be helpful if we begin to look at the events in our own lives, in our Christian tradition and in the life of Jesus. We look at those people who can show us that to discern, and to grow in discernment, we must adhere to the truth, and carry it out lovingly.

In this second phase, we will focus on leaving the 'world of the merchant', as Francis and Clare did, and letting go consciously. Thus, we may get some glimpses of what it can be like to become citizens of another kind of world. For the Christian tradition, this will be mainly the world of the Eucharist.

> For Francis, Eucharist is the reality of Christ among us, present in littleness and hiddenness, just as he was present to his apostles, just as he was present in the womb of the virgin. This humble, hidden presence of Jesus in Francis' midst, challenged him to respond by becoming what he sees.[3]

For Francis and Clare, 'seeing and becoming the mystery of Christ became operative for them in the practice of the Eucharist and foot-washing in imitation of Christ'. In today's market economy, becoming is usually identified with acquiring and amassing, often to the point of insatiability. Security is identified with amassing possessions.

In this phase, we will look at how Francis came to see that the means to becoming truly human was in fact letting go of many things that appeared to him to have been important. In that sense, what originally was sweet became bitter, but conversely, what was bitter became sweet. That which had been sweet was found to be transient, but that which had been bitter was transformed into a source of joy.

'The avaricious person is perturbed about wealth, and he/she knows not when want will come upon him/her' (Prov 28.22). In a market economy, work is useless and burdensome if it does not obtain remuneration. Much of what is produced can be rendered apparently useless if plentiful: surplus goods, rather than being distributed, are burned and destroyed.

What makes Francis more relevant than ever today is his sensitivity with regard to the temptation of money. His financial prospects were good. We are in a capitalist economy and are affected by it. Success in lotteries is prayed for and dreamed about because money seems to give us endless possibilities: a nice home, a partner, plenty of opportunity for the family. Letting go of what money seemed to promise was part of the turning around for Francis, part of an alternative value system. He opted instead for a world where work was to be done as a service, where it became a joy to work with one's hands. In this way one could appreciate every created thing, be grateful for the blessings given through the fruits of the earth, through animals and through human beings as they tried to image their Creator in creativity, love and friendship. However, it would require a breaking of the old mould and becoming little, in order that humanity could receive and be empowered by true love and life, and enter into what is eternal. It meant, and still means, letting go of fame, reputation, expectations, power, money, security, remuneration and status. The book of Proverbs gives the leech as an example. The leech will draw blood – the life of the person

– and keep drawing the blood until both leech and person die. It was possible that people in certain circumstances might never have 'enough', never be satisfied.

> Three things are never satisfied; four never say enough – 'the earth never saturated with water, and the fire that never says enough, the nether world, and the barren womb. (Prov 13:15, 16)

The biblical writers cautioned against greed, and as a bulwark against it there were laws such as the law of gleaning, the law of first fruits and the law of limited growth (cf. Deut 26).

> Greed is poignant because it is always haunted and emptied by future possibility; it can never engage presence. However, the more sinister aspect of greed is its ability to sedate and extinguish desire. It destroys the natural innocence of desire, dismantles its horizons, and replaces them with a driven and atrophied possessiveness. This greed is now poisoning the earth and impoverishing its people. Having has become the sinister enemy of being.[4]

Francis expressed his horror of hoarding:

> And if by chance – which God forbid – it should happen that some brother has collected or is hoarding money or coins, with the sole exception of the needs of the sick as mentioned above, all the brothers are to consider him as a false brother and an apostate, a thief and robber, and as the one who held the purse (cf. Jn 12:6).[5]

For Francis, the origin of all sin stemmed from this desire to acquire, to possess. In his Second Admonition he says, 'For the person eats of the tree of knowledge of good, *who appropriates to himself his own will* and thus exalts himself over the good things which the Lord says and does in him.'[6]

Francis embarks on a journey in which he consistently discovers that he has many things of which he needs to let go. The more he lets go, the more he realises there is still more to let go of. We are reminded of his exhortation, 'Up until this, we have done nothing.' He was in debt to the Creator, and the debt was infinite.

> It may seem a paradox to say that a man may be transported with joy to discover that he is in debt, but this is only because in commercial cases the creditor does not generally share the transports of joy, especially when the debt is by hypothesis, infinite and therefore unrecoverable.[7]

What was true in Eden and at Sinai is also true in everyday experience. Sin takes advantage of the law, perverting its function, so that the commandment designed to expose and check covetousness, actually produces in me all kinds of covetousness. Were it not for sin, the commandment would have promoted life, but because of sin, the commandment promotes death. Sin's blatant misuse of God's holy law reveals its true character as 'a dynamic overlord that induces a spirit of rebellion against God and of disobedience to his commandments. As with the offer of salvation in the first place, we are totally dependent on God's grace for transformation, especially as we face the possibility of death. There is no programme of sanctification or glorification we can effect by ourselves. There is no way of hurrying up God's work in us. We are called to live the sanctified life with faith, repentance and obedience, trusting the Spirit to continue and complete his great work of glorification'.[8]

Poverty

> The true source of Clare's and Francis' poverty is their spiritual and mystical experience of God as loving Father. Their poverty is both a consequence of this spiritual experience and the means of expressing and preserving it.[9]

The realisation that we are totally indebted to God should not cause fear. It should, in fact, liberate us. God is not seeking some kind of payback. We are called instead to be generous so that others can experience God's generosity through us. Here,

> ...the truth is... that the whole world has, or is, only one good thing: It is a bad debt.[10]

Jesus accepted being wounded, being poor, giving, sharing, serving, being vulnerable, being despised, making mistakes, being a failure, being insignificant. Francis chose that same path. To wash the feet of others, as in the example of Jesus, was for Francis and Clare a chosen path, a decision to walk the way of freedom, joy and liberation. It was a sacred path, a gift of life. Francis also wished to wash the feet of all those whom he regarded as nauseating, frightening, threatening or insulting. It was not a case of *trying* to love. Rather, it was letting go, so that God could find space to love in him, and he could recognise in the other the God who was present. In spite of all the events in his life and his many decisions to turn away from the 'world of the merchant', it was when he accepted what was nauseating to him and experienced the joy of liberation from his inner prison, that he could say that he had left the world of sin, spiritual imprisonment and darkness. He experienced enlightenment. Transformation followed. Francis, in his care of the lepers,

> …washed their feet, and bound up their sores, drawing off the pus and wiping them clean. He was extraordinarily devoted to them and he kissed their wounds, he was soon to play a part worthy of the Good Samaritan in the Gospel.[11]

Clare also came to the same discovery. In her Second Letter to Agnes of Prague we find her stating:

> Look upon Him Who became contemptible for you and follow Him, making yourself contemptible in the world for Him.[12]

Today, there are many serious diseases from which we would hope to be spared. All of us have our pet horrors, perhaps a disease that causes slow bodily disintegration, or a disease that evokes not sympathy, but quite the opposite. Leprosy was such a disease. Were we to live in the Middle Ages, our constant prayer might well be, 'God grant that I may never become a leper', or even, 'God grant that I may never meet a leper'.

To the romantic young Francis, the sight of lepers would have been a cause for alarm mingled with revulsion. Feared as leprosy was in the Middle Ages, it was also associated with a variety of sins. Lepers were banished from the town and a funeral service was held for them, so that they were buried in thought and in deed.

> Its chronic, prolonged character, the deforming effect which it might have on the appearance, the ulceration which sometimes involved the eyes and caused blindness,

the neurological changes bringing paralysis or weakness of muscles, the loss in some cases of fingers and toes…. All these made the leper an object of terror as well as pity, and so there was a social necessity to remove them.[13]

To embrace what is bitter and find it sweet is certainly a reversal of what we normally experience. For us, as for Francis, to trust in the activity of a God who loves us is a decision to allow our lives to be transformed. God surrounds with love what in us is limitation, vulnerability and weakness, so as to evoke in us strength, dignity, independence. Yet we often try to evade this love.

Dorothy Day pointed out that we are often prepared to hand over what should be our responsibilities to someone else:

In our country, we have revolted against the poverty and hunger of the world. Our response has been characteristically American: We have tried to clean up everything, build bigger and better shelters and hospitals. Here, hopefully misery was to be cared for in an efficient and orderly way. Yes, we have tried to do much, with Holy Mother the State taking over more and more responsibility for the poor. But charity is only as warm as those who administer it. When bedspreads may not be ruffled by the crooked limbs of age and bedside tables will not hold the clutter of those who try to make a home around them with little possessions, we know that we are falling short in our care of others.[14]

While the setting of these words is the USA, the same applies all over the developed world. Because our resistance to God is immense, we generally do not receive God's gifts. We still have not left the world of sin.

Francis' early companions also found it difficult to embrace the leper. Michael de la Bedoyere says that in the Second Rule, 'also suppressed was the reference to the care of lepers, a reference which must have been instinctive to him, because otherwise he could never have been the Francis we knew'.[15] Francis' early followers cared for the lepers precisely because the lepers were the most marginalised. In 1345 the Bishop of Spoleto affirmed that the Lepers' Hospice of San Lazaro Valloncello was founded by Francis for the use of the poor who were ill, and above all for the 'friars minor afflicted with leprosy'. 'Many brothers of the Order of Friars Minor, infected with such sickness, still remain.'[16] As Francis wrote in the Testament, this transformation from bitterness to sweetness was crucial. It was as if he preferred being with the lepers to being with people without leprosy. Every age and every society has its marginalised. 'In the second half of the thirteenth century, groups which were outcast from society were lepers, Jews and prostitutes. They all had to wear badges.'[17] Perugia's statute of 1279 condemned women who had sexual relationships with lepers to be flogged and dragged through the cities and suburbs, to have their noses cut off, and to be banished permanently from the city.[18]

In one of the great tales of the time, 'Tristan and Isolde', King Mark wants to put his wife, Isolde, to death because she has betrayed him. The head of a group of lepers shouts at the king, 'Give her to us. Death is too easy for her. Let us ravish her and that will be punishment enough.' The king duly concurs and gives Isolde to the lepers. However, the knight, Tristan, famous for his care of the defenceless and vulnerable, saves Isolde. He has no problem in viciously beating aside the lepers because to him they are of no value. Tristan would not have been expected to treat them as human beings, to be merciful or forgiving. In doing what he did to save Isolde, he was truly the knight in people's eyes. In contrast, Francis realised that true knighthood was based in a deep humility that was sensitive to the plight of every creature.

Hermann Schaluck OFM, General of the Order of Friars Minor, wrote to the Friars Minor:

> We wish in this way to experience an ongoing exodus, constantly engaged in a journey of liberation and in a *permanent process* which is both individual and social (#75). In this way, we will be made capable of *contemplating* God, *hearing* God's appeals in the midst of history, *recognising* the divine presence in the poor....[19]

Once we accept this, the sign of the Lord's favour will begin to be operative in us, to make us free and pure of heart so that we align ourselves in our rightful place alongside 'the leper', the poor, and all outside the margins of society in our time. What happened in Francis' life can then happen in ours.

> At the same time I admonish and exhort the brothers in the Lord Jesus Christ that they be aware of all pride, vainglory, envy, avarice (cf. Lk 12:15), cares and worries of this world (cf. Mt 13:22), detraction and complaint. And those who are illiterate should not be eager to learn. Instead, let them pursue what they must desire above all things: *to have the Spirit of the Lord and his holy manner of working.*[20]

Those who gathered round Francis and followed his way of life were advised by him:

> And wherever the brothers may be together or meet (other) brothers, let them give witness that they are members of

one family. And let each one confidently make known his need to the other, for if a mother has such care and love for her son, born according to the flesh (cf. I Thess 2:7), should not someone love and care for his brother according to the Spirit even more diligently? And if any of them becomes sick, the other brothers should serve him as they would wish to be served themselves (Mt 7:12).[21]

This context of family was important for Francis and Clare. Letting go in order to accept what was given by God made them brothers and sisters of all creation. Francis and Clare recognised providence, and for them there was no such thing as chance. God was over all and in all. In this perspective Clare called the members of her community 'poor sisters'.[22] Jean Francois Godet comments:

Lesser brothers and poor sisters, expresses therefore a programme of life which is qualified not only by the following of Christ but also by a certain type of interpersonal relationship. Francis did not call his companions, 'friends, comrades, monks, religious'; he called them brothers. Clare, choosing from among different possibilities of the same type, called her companions sisters. This means that for Clare as for Francis, *the relationship of fraternity is fundamental and primary.*[23]

Even the office of leader in the sisterhood/brotherhood is exercised in poverty. In Admonition 4 we read:

Let no one appropriate to himself the role of being over others. I did not come to be served but to serve (cf. Mt 10:28), says the Lord. Those who are placed over others should glory in such an office only as much as they would were they assigned the task of washing the feet of the brothers. And the more they are upset about their office being taken from them than they would be over the loss of the office of [washing feet], so much do they store up treasure to the peril of their soul (cf. Jn 12:6).[24]

Public Acclaim

Fear of men, anxiety about one's own well-being, drives away the fear of God: the fear of God drives away the fear of men and anxiety about our own existence. The fear of God arises in us at the same time as joy and gratitude for the love of God. It is the fear not to stand on the side of the Protector of the weak, but against him on the side of the strong, who live at the cost of the weak. It is the fear of perhaps having the powerful of the world on our side, but God against us.[25]

We look over our shoulders quite frequently before we make a decision. Francis crossed many boundaries and ceased to take account of the expectations of others. During his lifetime his great vision appeared in danger of being compromised by possible divisiveness, with some of his brothers going in a different direction from him. He resigned as Minister General of the Order. He did not seek to appropriate even this office to himself. It was God's will and so he had to let go. It was more important to leave matters in God's hands than to try to control the process himself.

People who follow Francis' way 'must rejoice when they live among people [who are considered to be] of little worth and who are looked down upon among the poor and the powerless, the sick and the lepers, and the beggars by the wayside'.[26]

Francis in his poverty let go of his respectability. He described himself as *le jongleur de Dieu.*

> He had also been at one time a troubadour, but a jongleur was not the same thing as a troubadour, even if the same man were both a troubadour and a jongleur. More often, I believe, they were separate men as well as separate trades. In many cases, apparently, the two men would walk the world together like companions in arts. The jongleur was properly a joculator, or jester; sometimes he was what we would call a juggler. There was to be found, ultimately, in such service, a freedom almost amounting to frivolity. It was comparable to the condition of the jongleur, because it almost amounted to frivolity. The jester could be free when the knight was rigid; it was possible to be a jester in the service, which is perfect freedom.[27]

The parables of Jesus Christ were intended to challenge prevailing attitudes and codes of conduct. The parable concerning the Samaritan helping a victim of robbery and abuse is a telling one. To have a Jewish priest tend a 'wounded' Samaritan may be unexpected, but to have a Samaritan being ethically superior to a Levite or priest was certainly startling. Forgiveness is unconditional and there can be no limit placed on generosity. The most vulnerable are to be cared for and protected, as they are indeed the most precious.

Change: The Institution and the System

Francis and Clare in their individual lives started a revolution by the decisions they made. A thousand such decisions would go a long way towards changing the face of this earth. Their way of life is a challenge to all of us, particularly in those areas where we have created financial, sociological and ecological imbalances that result in some barely ekeing out an existence, while others accrue more than they need.

> It is a challenge not only to the capitalist system of the west; it challenges equally the state capitalism of the east. Antonio Gramci is perhaps the most outstanding Italian mind of our century to have challenged both, and he deserves to be heard and considered: 'Despite the changing face of history, every social movement that matters has found one thing. It grows out of the economic structure that is already in being, and that structure determines the way it develops. But then there are already established ways of thinking, and these make it seem as if any new development is part of an uninterrupted process of history, and that puts even the most complicated and radical changes in the social and political forms into a manageable perspective'.[28]

> Francis looks like a pious bubble upon the sea of events. The movement which he founded makes him matter. His onslaught upon the money-making activities of his father is not just a freak. It is, and remains, a serious challenge to our subservience – east and west – to the god of economic growth.[29]

Sisterhood/brotherhood (fraternity) does not come about as a result of the type of service or apostolate in which groups engage. With regard even to religious community, Adrian Van Kaam states:

> If pressure groups do not deeply understand the essential character of a participative religious community, and thereby the respect they must develop for each fellow religious and his possible inspiration, they may be inclined

to identify such common enterprises with the religious community itself.[30]

With Francis and Clare, it was only when they discovered the pathway of Jesus Christ and walked in his footsteps that sisterhood/brotherhood, peace/reconciliation and justice ensued. The humility involved in the Incarnation was the key to opening the gate of mature and true humanity for all.

Only the 'good news' saves, in all the aspects that saving and salvation can mean. We can only solve the problem of unjust structures for the poor when we, by becoming poor, join with them. Francis and Clare well understood the promise, the reality and the mission.

The natural trend of today's society of social upward mobility is the wrong direction. No wonder Jesus, Clare and Francis disturb us, as their direction is downward – incarnation to be with the leper, the 'non-person', the one who counts for nothing in the social hierarchy.

No barriers existed for Francis and Clare – they had open hearts to all. Francis sat down with the leper and shared the same table. Clare and the sisters ate only food that had been begged for by the friars. Our poverty, chastity, obedience, sacrifices and promises are meaningless unless we take God seriously.

No known human relationship or social binding can compare with the intimacy of the Eucharist: actually partaking of the life of Jesus Christ. Through the Eucharist, we also partake in the life of every human being, since to partake in the power of Jesus Christ is also to partake in his service. We serve our brothers and sisters, especially those who are weaker, whatever their circumstances. Parents will often spend more time and energy with a dysfunctional or weak child, as that is the area of greatest need. Their presence is there for all the family, but it is more regularly to be found with the person who needs it most. We cannot miss out if we spend time with those most in need of the Creator's care, help and compassion. If we never spend time with them, then 'Where is God in our lives?'.

Francis and Clare of Assisi used the concept of motherhood as the human experience most likely to express accurately the nature of this bond in terms of commitment, empathy and belonging. The sister or brother whom I mistrust, dislike, reject or belittle, is really the measure of how much I genuinely partake of the Eucharist.

The desire in us for communion and oneness is not diminished by withdrawal or death experiences. When we grow and change our focus, we experience periods of transition. In solitude, in the desert, we will struggle with the forces that impede us from coming to terms with who we are, and who we are in relation to others.

In our desire to begin, we can overcome doctrinal differences if in pastoral practice we recognise the common ground we share – our desire to care for and be one with the marginalised. There are so many areas that require our common understanding: bereavement, addiction, care of the sick and awareness of those most misunderstood and rejected by society. Jesus Christ overcame the limits of the Judaism of his time. Francis overcame the limits of traditional Christianity. Our sense of sisterhood/brotherhood, our sense of oneness among ourselves and others must be discovered. What we have in common with other world faiths must be explored. The oneness depicted in the creation story of Adam and Eve in the garden must be explored in order that, like Francis divesting himself of everything at his death, our nakedness will again enable our communion with creation.

We can let go of the slavery of consumerism, the exploitation of persons and groups, the privileged positions we hold onto with regard to our relationships with other people, and our exploitation and insensitive domination of the earth. The anguish of Jesus, the anguish of God the Creator, is a pain that is part of love and part of creation, and for that reason is also a part of the death that eventually will give way to resurrection, '…but not a hair on your head will be destroyed' (Lk 21:18).

Every created particle is due reverence, as ultimately all is related to the Creator who conserves and preserves all things in existence. The compassion that is God goes beyond human rights. Francis and Clare wished to share in that compassion, so clearly expressed in the life of Jesus Christ. It is ultimately our mission, our fulfilment and our peace.

Living out of compassion, we gain the ability to see beyond the cross, to resurrection and fruitfulness. We also get the ability to see in our inconveniences and crosses the inevitable fruitfulness of love. Envy, hatred, jealousy and fear bring destruction, as is evidenced in so many parts of the world where injustice flourishes and wars are waged. But love can only bring a healing of such situations. Out of this arises gratitude, for life, for the promise, for our destiny as Francis expressed it in his Canticle of Creatures. Although at the end of his life he was blind and in great pain, he was not overcome by those destructive forces. Time and nature enable creative love to place blossoms and spectacular growth even in the most barren of deserts. Love means letting go of what seems important to us in order to let the Creator be – letting love be in charge.

The lives of our brothers and sisters, the global fraternity, is the food God gives us, the bread of life. In our shared life we can have 'twelve baskets' to spare. Building unity over the whole earth is the host presented to the father of the universe. In the hands of Jesus Christ we are all called into newness of life and to be life-giving for others. We all come to life, and it is from the hands of Christ that we are invited to 'take and eat'.

> Whatever you ask in my name, I will do, so as to glorify the Father in the Son. (Jn 14: 12-13)

> Where ethnic conflicts of all kinds tear nations apart and create situations of high tension, we ought to be promoters of peaceful concord, even if this means accepting initiatives which require great courage and upholding positions which are openly inspired by the gospel and the 'new commandment' of mutual love.[31]

For Francis and Clare, true sisterhood and brotherhood led them to the realm of harmony and peace, of friendship with all of creation. The words of Julian of Norwich in a later century, the fourteenth, sum up what Francis and Clare experienced:

> See, I am God. See, I am in all things. See, I never leave my hands off my works, nor ever shall, through all eternity. See, I lead all things to the end I have prepared for them. I do this by the same wisdom, and love, and power through which I made them. How can anything be done that is not done well?[32]

PHASE III – PEACE

In Christ, the cosmic renewal which is to characterise the eschatological era is already effected. The risen body of Jesus is the first cell of the New Cosmos. In Him the Spirit has already taken possession of matter, as He will one day take possession of the entire creation at the Parousia when Christ will definitively recapitulate all things in Himself... by the mystical union of Baptism and the Eucharist. With Him they have risen from the dead.[1]

What about unity of Action? Look at a beehive. The bees are governed by an instinct, acting unconsciously by a compulsion which strictly controls all their acts, without leaving any scope for chance or whim. It is the same with the other animals; having a personal destiny dependent on what they do, they have no freedom. We, however, made to the image of God and so personally immortal and free are to bring about, consciously and through love, something analogous to what the bees do – namely, to form a single body, the Body of Christ. The spiritual unity of all people in Christ – has to be established, not by physical fusion and loss of personality, but by that love in which, uniting himself to others, each becomes most truly himself. The Body of Christ is not a hive, but a city of free people, willingly harmonising with one another in love.[2]

The way of Francis and Clare was one of peace and healing. No one can claim to be a person of faith in Jesus Christ, i.e. a religious person, if destructive or violent methods are intended to be used to achieve a goal. In this regard Arturo Paoli says:

> To be religious is to give your life so that the world may be more beautiful, more just, more at peace; it is to prevent egotistical and self-serving ends from disrupting this harmony of the whole.[3]

Francis and Clare were able to walk in the shoes of all with whom they came in contact. Thus, for them, the notion of anyone as enemy was eliminated because they were already one in sisterhood and brotherhood with all, including enemies.

In Phase I, Humility, we saw that it is essential to experience the God who gives us our value. We are all equal in the eyes of God and our value comes from God. Otherwise, if we look only at each other, even in terms of equality, other forces can enter in, such as the avarice, envy and jealousy to which Francis referred. The propensity for this to happen is there in all human history, as shown in the story of Cain and Abel. We also saw that humility is vital if we are not to become enemies to our sisters and brothers.

We are used to dwelling in a world with thousands of mirrors, constantly seeing ourselves and seeing how others view us. Meditating (prayer) is a definitive smashing of all mirrors. It is looking, not at reflections of things, or at reflections of ourselves, but into the reality that is God.

In Phase II, Sisterhood/Brotherhood, we realise that it is in service that we recognise our relationship as sisters and brothers, and that additionally we are called to take responsibility for each other by also being mothers and fathers to each other.

The Eucharist, given as bread for the journey, should unite all our brokenness in such a way that it makes a united people. God is a reconciler. Where we are willing instruments, we become bridge-builders. The Lord will always guide us.

Even in marriage, Billy Graham talks of 'Happy Incompatibles':

Ruth and I don't have a perfect marriage, but we have a great one. How can I say two things that seem so contradictory? In a perfect marriage, everything is always the finest and best imaginable; like a Greek statue, the proportions are exact and the finish is unblemished. Who knows any human beings like that: for a married couple to expect perfection in each other is unrealistic. We learned that even before we were married.

Being human, not one of us will ever have a relationship with another person that doesn't have a wrinkle or a wart on it somewhere. The unblemished ideal exists only in 'happily ever after' fairytales. I think that there is some merit to a description I once read of a married couple as 'happily incompatible'. Ruth likes to say, 'If two people agreed on everything, one of them is unnecessary.' The sooner we accept that as a fact of life, the better we will be able to adjust to each other and enjoy togetherness. 'Happily incompatible' is a good adjustment.[4]

Francis and Clare understood the intimate union made possible by the love of God, a union grounded in reality. For Clare, Francis was the concrete channel through which she knew and loved God. In her Testament she said that 'Francis was our pillar [of strength] and after God, our one consolation and support'. It was this human love that ensured that Clare avoided the dangers of excessive exaltation and of religious ecstasy. The friendship was real. It was human. It was born out of the reality of their mutual love of God. Consequently they cared for one another and were compassionate towards one another as Christ is towards all of us.

The Eucharist was of paramount significance to Francis and Clare. They saw it not only as prayerful silence but also as activity, as a way of being, as a social self-definition, as a way of determining relationships among sisters and brothers. Francis summarises his theology in two texts: 'Admonition 1' and the 'Letter to the Entire Order'. The first Admonition speaks of the Eucharist in an Incarnational context:

> See, daily He humbled Himself (cf. Phil 2:8) as when He came from the royal throne (Wis 18:15) into the womb of the Virgin, daily He comes to us in a humble form; daily He comes down from the bosom of the Father (cf. Jn 1:18) upon the altar in the hands of the priest. And as He appeared to the holy apostles in true flesh, so now He reveals Himself to us in the sacred bread. And as they saw only His flesh by means of their bodily sight, yet believed Him to be God as they contemplated Him with the eyes of faith, so, as we see bread and wine with (our) bodily eyes, we too are to see and firmly believe them to be His most holy Body and Blood living and true. And in this way the Lord is always with His faithful, as He Himself says: Behold I am with you even to the end of the world (cf. Mt 28:20).[5]

In the 'Letter to the Entire Order', Francis spoke of the responsibility of the brothers to this great gift of God's presence:

> Oh, admirable heights and sublime lowliness, sublime humility, Oh humble sublimity. That the Lord of the universe, God and the Son of God, so humbled himself for our salvation that he hides himself in the little form of bread! Look, brothers at the humility of God and pour out your hearts before him. Humble yourselves, as well, that you may be exalted by him. Therefore, hold back nothing of yourselves by yourselves, so that he who gives himself totally to you, may receive you totally.[6]

Strengthened by bread for the journey in the Eucharist, the mission of the friars is to build a better world and to bring peace.

> The biblical doctrine of the Kingdom of God, when viewed through the optic of the primacy of Christ, is a message about the eternal significance of creation and of human efforts to create a better world. In this we discover a genuine religious motivation for us to identify with all human efforts, to overcome the obstacles to the coming of the Kingdom. In the light of this doctrine, Christians, inspired by the example of Francis of Assisi, should be able to say with abiding truth that they love the world. Their love for the world need not replace their love for God.[7]

We saw in Phase II, Sisterhood/Brotherhood, that for Francis to become a lesser brother meant becoming one with those most despised in his own society, those who, for him, were objects of disgust, the lepers. With Clare, even though she was a beautiful noblewoman, it meant a total change of lifestyle, the cutting of her hair, and putting on poor garments. If we are to take the way of Francis and Clare, who followed in the footsteps of Jesus, we also are called to overcome our natural repugnances and to welcome all, including those whom society tends to marginalise. We must refer constantly to the position of the leper in medieval society to understand and appreciate what it means to be able to identify the marginalised, and therefore to know the people towards whom we should move in our hearts. These are truly our brothers and our sisters. Welcoming them into our lives is allowing the life of Jesus to enter into us.

Francis made the incarnation real and immediate at Greccio, and he composed a real crib scene, '...and out of Greccio is made a new Bethlehem.'[8] Ewert Cousins, a distinguished historian of spirituality and mysticism, has labelled Francis' contribution 'the mysticism of the historical event'.[9]

> The variety of mystical experience that Francis seeks for himself and others at Greccio begins with the historical and concrete dimensions of life. Francis wants us not to remember the events, so much as to experience it for ourselves. One way to begin is to try to recall and even 'stage' as much as possible how the original event looked to those who were participants. So, in our presence at an event such as the incarnation, we come to perceive God's plan for salvation as present because God reveals himself in history. Beginning with our entering into an event such as the nativity and perceiving God's plan, we are led to union with God. As Cousins points out, the mysticism of the historical event is related to nature mysticism. Our union with nature or with the historical event, 'becomes a mode of God's communication of himself to us...' and of our union with him by perceiving his presence in the physical world.[10]

The Evangelists and the followers of the early Church were human beings with the limitations of human bias. For Francis, however, the accounts of the birth of Jesus according to the tradition of both Matthew and Luke afforded him the opportunity of getting to understand and know more about the Creator's communication with creation. He wished to hear and experience the cry of a needy child at Christmas. It was an opportunity to try to experience a God who smiled and breathed and cried. He wished to contemplate the mother and her responses to the child who needed to be fed. Mary was able to touch flesh of her flesh and recognise in her baby the shape of the mouth and the eyes that resembled hers.

Luke and Matthew were, to Francis, artists who communicated a sense of a God who became vulnerable so that we might learn the language of caring, the language of compassion. No wonder Francis wished his companions to act as mothers to one another.

Carols at Christmas can sometimes open up a tradition that illustrates the wonder of the birth:

> On this day's morning, as a tiny Child; a tiny Child,
> The root of Jesse was born, a tiny Child;
> The Mighty come from Bozra.
> The Lawgiver once on Sinai.
> The Atonement gained on Calvary, a tiny Child;
> a tiny Child,
> Sucking the breast of Mary, a tiny Child.
> Came the living water of Ezekiel, on Mary's knee;
> on Mary's knee,
> And Daniel's true Messiah, on Mary's knee;
> The wise child of Isaiah,
> The promise given to Adam.
> The Alpha Omega, on Mary's knee; on Mary's knee,
> In a stall in Bethlehem, Judah, on Mary's knee.[11]

This Plygain carol replaced the old Latin hymns and is part of the Welsh tradition. It brings into focus the wonder of the incarnation, as Francis saw it.

A good use of the historical data with regard to leprosy in the Middle Ages will enable all participants to be part of the society of Francis, whereby they will understand and appreciate what it really meant to make a decision to work with and be one with the lepers. It will allow for an understanding of what kind of response might be deemed 'Franciscan' today. It also opens the way to be one with the world that is alien to us, the world of which we are in fear, so that we may accept everything in the universe.

> Now we can explicitly affirm that these stays at the leprosarium essentially constituted the novitiate for the first Friars Minors, as the indispensable condition for being accepted into the fraternity. We have already pointed out that the love of this fraternal service to the lepers is the measure for advancement into the way of perfection. It is this dominating dream of Francis that re-emerges during his last days, when in God's light, he once again sees more perfectly the essential things of his life and he feels the desire to begin again. 'We ardently desire to return to the humble origins of his evangelical journey, and lighthearted with new hope for the immensity of love, he proposed once again to bring his body into the initial obedience of the spirit…. He wanted to return to servicing the lepers, and to be held in contempt, just as he used to be.'[12]

It was a calling to a totally different understanding of life, a call to an alternative vision of living. It was new, it was a risk, 'a vocation in terms of the generosity which inspired the response to the divine call and the constancy with which he followed it through'.[13] Francis was so much one with the marginalised that he could always truthfully say that he was nothing but a beggar in need of help from everybody. Therefore, because he was no threat, he was an instrument of peace in his way of life, and this way of life continues to make its impact today.

Francis and Clare were both witnesses to the mission of Jesus Christ. *Their commitment was to God's plan in history and in everyday reality.* Their vision was broad as God's is broad.

True cleverness means breadth of vision, and breadth of vision is the freedom to lift one's gaze beyond the pressures of today into an enduring perspective. True cleverness is thinking of the whole. That is the freedom of my breaking the fetters of my own interest, taking into equal consideration with my own, the interest of others, realising that I am only a part of a whole, and thinking from that viewpoint. This cleverness is a mode of freedom. To believe means truly to reckon with the reality of the living God. It is the reality of the living God that creates the connection between seed and harvest.[14]

We enslave ourselves with self-made barriers and we suffocate ourselves with an illusory way of living.

Through the coupling of incarnation and liberation, it is possible to re-conceive our understanding of human freedom, as 'freedom for', not only 'freedom from.' In effect, it engages the theological imagination in a consideration of what it means for the human person to be free for God and free for good.[15]

As a conclusion to this programme, the Canticle, the account of Francis' death, and particularly the Peace Prayer attributed to him, need to be part of the spiritual tools that participants take with them in a new way. Francis' spirit continues to live on among his followers who have handed on that spirit.

This peace, which Christ passes on to us and which the world cannot give, is the merging together of closeness with God, harmony with other people and all creation, and integrity within ourselves. The reality of peace occurs when we have changed our attitudes and actions. As instruments of peace, which we saw in Phase I on Humility, and in Phase II on Sisterhood/Brotherhood, we allow God to come to speak to us, and we listen. We avoid divisiveness and personal self-destruction and become life-givers through ascertaining and accepting God's life plan of holiness for us.

> Finally, my brothers and sisters, your thoughts should be wholly directed to all that is true, all that deserves respect, all that is honest, pure, admirable, decent, virtues that are worthy of praise. Live according to what you have learned and accepted, what you have heard me say and seen me do. Then, will the God of peace be with you. (Phil 4:8-9)

Our own knowledge has to be transformed into faith, so that when we are tempted to surrender to despair, cynicism or depression, we will realise that life is with us. God has given life meaning in Jesus Christ. In spite of difficulties, we are given a meaning that can turn despair into hope.

We can transform our darkness into light. Often we are very negative in fearing our own power to destroy the world. We can transform bitterness into sweetness. God is on our side, and God is a God of life.

Even our understanding of death can be very negative. This was not so for Francis. Having completed the journey from bitterness to sweetness, he saw death as a passage from the joy that he experienced here to the eternal joy that would embrace everything and everyone and never end.

It would be good to ask for this kind of faith in prayer, and allow ourselves to admit to God that there are times when we do not trust. When we are frightened or insecure we do not like to forget ourselves because we feel that nobody else will think about us. We can make use of the Peace Prayer and allow that prayer to help us. In our petitions and prayers of intercession, we need to ask of God nothing but God himself. We can ask God to help us be consolers and to understand. Our natural craving is to be understood and to be consoled. We need to learn to respect every human being, to know that love gives life, and to know that love is what life is about. In our giving, we receive. It is in forgetting ourselves that we find ourselves. It is in our ability to pardon that in fact we are pardoned. It is very difficult at times to see this. We can express that difficulty in our petitions to God. There is no peace without forgiveness, and there is no eternal life without death. We find that this is true of all life, with the myriad examples in nature of dying and resurgence of life. The leaning to self-centredness, self-indulgence and petty judgemental attitudes that can dictate the tenor of much of our lives is meant to be transformed into the scriptural 'abundant life', which means charity, buoyancy, and knowing eternal life in the kernel of the present.

It is not a question of being peace-keepers, but peace-makers, who relate to each other, who understand, who dismantle barriers. Regardless of people's response we can, ourselves, try always to promote understanding. We can try always to give life and to know what life-giving actions are: to counsel the doubtful; to instruct the ignorant; to help people to see their mistakes in order that they may be free; to bear wrongs patiently; to forgive offences; to comfort the afflicted; to pray for everybody. So, we move as pilgrims and strangers through a world that is familiar but that always needs reconciliation. That world and its aspirations for reconciliation is ultimately on our side, because God is on our side.

The Franciscan mission of peace and charity is the unfolding of a reality given to us by Jesus Christ. It is recognised and actualised by our own conversion to a free and open embracing of the gospel, by our risk-taking with discernment, by our honest commitment to justice, and by our self-giving service to one another. This peace and charity is both a promise and a pledge. It is God's gift and our task.[16]

How can we become gatherers, reconcilers and builders instead of destroyers? How can we deal with brokenness, limitations and sickness? How can we become at one with ourselves and decide to be open to the power and also the humility of God? How can we have a positive attitude towards death, seeing it as a passage from one realm of existence to another? How can we learn to trust that all those whom we love will be taken care of through God's ongoing providence?

Reflecting on the Peace Prayer, we can ask: how do we change hatred into love? As we saw in Phase I, we start by recognising our own lovableness. When we jettison that hatred of others that manifests itself in disgust, resentment, rash judgement or denigration, or that hatred of God whereby we blame the divine for the faults and failures of the human condition, then we can allow ourselves to be transformed.

What kind of wounds have we sustained that need to be touched by pardon? We can wound ourselves by not caring for ourselves properly in a physical, mental or spiritual way. If allowed, God can call forth in us God's very own qualities. But injuring others by destructive words, detrimental behaviour or damaging thoughts frustrates the action of God, who can only give life, who does not destroy. We can have a sense of false inferiority or false superiority. We may project onto other people our own difficulties. We may believe that we can analyse and sum up people's behaviour or their intentions, when only God can do that. We can also have a very superficial knowledge of who God really is, which does not allow God to be God, the merciful and loving One. If we have been wounded, we can turn this into pardon. We can transform error into truth. We can deal with all illusions we have about ourselves. Sometimes sickness and the kind of event that brought Francis to his senses can bring us to our senses too.

We cannot put a time or limit to the working of God's mercy. We are all enriched by the help of one another in understanding and appreciating the merciful God. This requires going apart, as Jesus and Francis did, away from the people who will convince us otherwise. We are then giving ourselves the chance to liberate ourselves from illusory importance in a world that is transient, a world that wants to cling to mere chronological time, which is nothing more that a human concept, instead of entering into the eternal stream of God's time.

In Luke's Gospel, God is portrayed as one who is deeply concerned and searches for the sheep that has strayed from the flock. The bringing home of the stray is uniquely longed for. What to us may be assessed as having little value, to God is without price. We are called to discern as God discerns, to value as God values each one of us (cf. Lk 15:3-7).

Often, because of our fears, we fail to see our world as friendly or to recognise in it all the beauty, presence and power of the Creator. Francis and Clare were imbued with constant awareness of the presence of God within and around them.

Francis often invoked Saint Michael the Archangel as protector, since he was certain of help on all sides by the angels of the Lord.

> Learning to work with the angels is to begin living more and more in a different current of time, and to recognise besides the current of time that extends from the past into the present and toward the future, there is an additional current of time that comes from the future into the present. Learning to attend to this time stream, we experience more of what we can be, rather than thinking of ourselves in terms of the influences of the past. The angels, I think, 'ride' this stream of time, and their concern

(particularly guardian angels) is guiding us in our destiny. Our destiny comes to us from the future. There are, of course, all of the effects of the past – heredity, memory, conditioning, talents and abilities, and these too work powerfully in our lives. The angels, however, are primarily concerned with our future individually, as well as with the future of humanity and of the future of the world. Working with the angels implies learning to care for what is not yet present, but what is coming to be.[17]

Thoughtful men, once escaped from the blinding influences of traditional prejudice, will find in the lowly stock whence man has sprung, the best evidence of the splendour of his capacities, and will discern in his long progress through the past, a reasonable ground of faith in his attainment of a noble future.[18]

Christ wanted men to see, to see far and to see truly. To get that kind of vision requires avoidance of hypocrisies and group prejudice, which distort the vision and make men imagine they see what is not really there.[19]

In the face of suffering, one has no right to turn away, not to see. In the face of injustice, one may not look the other way. When someone suffers and it is not you, he comes first. His very suffering gives him priority... . To watch over a man who grieves is a more urgent duty than to think of God.[20]

The Creator's compassion does not ignore the least of creation, the hair of the head, or the simplest life form, or the apparent lifelessness of matter. The spirituality of Francis encompasses this.

Francis' life represents the flowering of the ecological promise of the classical Christian ethos. The mind and life of Francis are shaped... by the metaphor of migration to a good land and the metaphor of fecundity. Francis climbs the mountain of God's creation in order to stand in universal solidarity with all God's creatures, both in this world and in the world to come, for which he so passionately yearns. Then he descends, as he perceived God's love always to be overflowing, in order to embrace all the creatures of God, not only the specially elected and specially blessed human creatures.[21]

Francis and Clare longed for eternal life, but both viewed life as a gift and all creation to be one great debt.

...a focus on gratitude for the gift of life rather than a longing for eternal life; an end to dualistic hierarchies, including human beings over nature; an appreciation for the individuality of all things rather than the glorification of human individualism; a sense of radical interrelatedness and interdependence with all that exists; the acceptance of responsibility for other forms of life and the ecosystem, as guardians and partners of the planet; the acknowledgement that salvation is physical as well as spiritual and hence, that sharing the basics of existence is a necessity; and, finally, the recognition that sin is the refusal to stay in our proper place – sin is, as it always has been understood in the Jewish and Christian traditions, living a lie.[22]

We are tempted to see the universe revolve around ourselves – what *I* want, what *I* hope for, what *I* fear. It doesn't! Each of us forms a part. There are other creatures who also have wants, fears and expectations, who are courageous, who value their independence, and who have a sense of their own worth. There is no entity, even in the darkest realms, outside the power and design of the Creator. We need to accept and come to know our place, the part we have to play. We need to know our relationship with the Creator and with one another. We need to join intimately with the heart of Christ so that we will have the capacity to know and love the depth, breath, and height of the heart of the Creator, who holds all things in being and around whom everything revolves.

To take the road of trust in life, to know that life is with us, and to believe in the fundamental goodness of all of creation, is to take the step of faith similar to Francis and Clare. It means discarding the baggage that feeds our insecurities, builds walls and creates lack of trust. This allows the deep springs of truth and life within us to be part of all that is life-giving in creation. We can be part of a process that bears fruit in time and eternity. It takes enduring patience, watchfulness and courage to let go of our deep-seated fears. We can read the signs of the times, the patterns of history. We need not take as a guide the instant interpretations of the happenings of the day. We need not see the 'bizarre' as the most adventurous and rewarding reality. We need not make premature judgements of people or current events. We need not see screaming headlines as the way, the truth and the life. Our future is already guaranteed. The Father loses nothing that the Son presents to him. We present, with the Son, in trust, the good we are and do. We present the bad we do as well, to be forgiven and transformed. All we are, we give.

To encourage and promote life and forgiveness/reconciliation is the only way in which we can limit the damage that results from our desire to play God. All sin, at the least, damages us. It can even destroy us. The life-giving Creator neither desires nor brings about any form of destruction. Jesus came to give life in abundance. He did not come to condemn. When we fail to keep in mind our creaturehood, we are rejecting reality.

To justify our behaviour and protest that it is superior to another's is to try to curtail the activity of the Creator to the limitations of creaturehood. This is sheer fantasy. All sin stems from this denial of the reality that God is God and we are creatures. This is the original relationship – all is gift.

To live is to live in trust as Christ did in the heart of creativity, peace, growth and fruitfulness. The active presence of the Creator in this life was the activity of the Father, i.e. Our Father. That Fatherhood is accepted by people who choose to live as Francis and Clare, guided by the Spirit on the pathway (journey) to Our Father and their Father, as full sisters and brothers of Jesus Christ.

Our 'world-view' will constantly change, as our vision will always need to expand and develop. It must constantly grow as it increasingly allows the vision and action of God in the world to be worked out through us. As Christ has become one with creation, all of creation's processes are animated by him. His love in response to the Father moves all of creation, under the guidance of the Spirit.

Our hearts need to be ready to endure the pain of expansion. To love with Jesus and Mary every human heart and every created entity, is to express what is truly human and to fulfil the longing of the human heart for God, and so to be possessed by God.

On that journey, the peace of our own little securities will be shattered. Our towers of Babel, no matter what religious title or altruistic name we might give them, will of necessity collapse.

Frank O'Connor, in one of his short stories 'My Oedipus Complex',[23] describes how he prayed with his mother for his father to return safe and well from the war, and also for a companion, a baby brother or sister. He was at peace then – his world was his mother and he seemed to be her world. The entry of his father and later a baby brother shattered his little world. No longer was he the centre of his mother's attention and, for a time, he could not handle it.

The Spirit of Truth shatters our illusory securities. The Spirit breathes through all of creation. In order to journey along the pathways of life in the way of Francis and Clare of Assisi, we need to yield up to the Spirit the illusions to which we cling, so that we can experience true peace and joy.

The true language of love was expressed in the life of Jesus Christ. That trust of the Creator and creation will be taught to us and given to us by the Spirit of Truth. It is real power, it is growth, it is not an illusion. We can do so much together to support and encourage this one language, one tongue, which unites and resonates with hidden chords in hearts of different cultures and different ways of life.

Through the ages there has been no shortage of witnesses to the power of love as shown by Jesus Christ, in spite of death and destruction. Easter confirms that love conquers and remains. The life and death of people like Francis and Clare of Assisi also witness to this. Christ is one with the poor and suffering till the end of the world. No power can overcome true love. Francis and Clare of Assisi discovered this and it proved to be the 'pearl of great price'. Their lives show us what is possible if we place our trust in God.

The more we allow love to take over, the more prejudice, envy and jealousy will disappear so that we can listen to life and other people with a heart that truly hears. The more unlimited our love becomes and the more we truly listen, the better we will understand other people's points of view and we will be enabled to walk in their shoes. Our judgements will become more comprehensive and balanced. Our decisions will then be invested with responsibility and insight. Our focus will be more real. We will become more magnanimous. We will begin to love as our Creator loves, unconditionally.

Clare and Francis did not choose comfort. They embraced the cross, the way of Jesus Christ. They pleased God rather than human beings. They wanted to serve rather than be served. It will always be difficult to accept that Jesus Christ was given the cross ultimately by us. Only the truth will set us free. We are called to spread the good news to others, to spread peace. Billy Graham says:

> If I had it to do over again, I would also avoid any semblance of involvement in partisan politics. On the whole, as I've already said, my primary concern in my contacts with political leaders has been as a pastor and spiritual counsellor, not as a political adviser. When a president of the United States, for example, wept in my presence, or knelt with me to pray, or privately unburdened his concerns about his family, I was not thinking about his political philosophy or his personality but about his need for God's help.
>
> And yet there have been times when I undoubtedly stepped over the line between politics and my calling as an evangelist. An evangelist is called to do one thing, and one thing only: to proclaim the Gospel. Becoming involved in strictly political issues or partisan politics inevitably dilutes the evangelist's impact and compromises his message. It is a lesson I wish I had learned earlier.[24]

For Francis and Clare, the pathway to Jesus was the following in his footsteps so that they could find him in the way he finds us. He emptied himself, taking the form of a slave, coming in human likeness (cf. Phil 2:7). God who is love became poor – love leads to self-emptying, letting go for the sake of another, embracing death, even death on a cross for the sake of the life of another (cf. Phil 2:7). Love leads to poverty. Poverty calls forth love. Our poverty can be the result of love and at the same time asks for love and compassion from others. Only Jesus, and his way of living, teaches us to love. Neither poverty nor wealth, only the life-giving spirit of the Creator, can teach us to love.

Jesus alone gives meaning to poverty and suffering. If the followers of Jesus Christ suffer as Christ suffered, they confidently expect relief and happiness to come to them in time. Certainly one day there will be no more tears, no more suffering, 'we shall see Him as he is' and 'we shall be like him' (1 Jn 3:2).

'Behold I tell you a mystery. We shall not all fall asleep, but we will be changed' (1 Cor 15:51). The preparation, the journey towards that final change, begins now in our individual processes of conversion. We all need to allow circumstances and events, God's time, God's way, constantly to transform our own models, our own world-views. Even then we will see only 'indistinctly as in a mirror', but then it will be 'face to face' (1 Cor 13:12).

> So we are ambassadors for Christ, since God is making his appeal through us; we entreat you on behalf of Christ, be reconciled to God. (2 Cor 5:17-20)

Franciscan tradition spells out the task clearly in 'The legend of the Three Companions'. 'Our calling is to heal wounds, to reunite those divided by enmity or misunderstanding, to lead back home those who have lost their way.'[25]

As individuals and as a group, it may appear a daunting task, but what God accomplished through Francis and Clare he can accomplish through us. With such a focus we will bear fruit with trust in the promise and possibility that we can make a better world.

Let us as a group bless each other from our hearts, as Paul blessed the Thessalonians: 'may the God of Peace make you whole and holy; and may you all be kept safe and blameless in spirit, soul and body for the coming of our Lord Jesus Christ (1 Thess 23).

PART THREE

RESOURCES FOR FACILITATORS

HUMILITY

Lady, holy Poverty, may the Lord protect you with your sister, holy Humility.

Lady, Holy Charity, may the Lord protect you with your sister, Holy Obedience.

Holy humility destroys pride, and all the people who are in the world, and all things that belong to the world.

Holy charity destroys every temptation of the devil and of the flesh, and every carnal fear.

Holy obedience destroys every wish of the body and of the flesh, and binds its mortified body to obedience of the Spirit, and to obedience of one's brother.[1]

The soul that has gazed on God (and felt its own inability to bring about its own transformation) does not need to reflect on its lowliness because there is no way the soul can deny it.[2]

KEY CONCEPTS
- God's Agenda
- Sense of Self
- Value to God
- Contemplation

Discussion 1
'The glory of God is the human person fully alive' (St Irenaeus). What might it mean to be 'fully human'?

The stars shine. They do so beautifully, which is what they are created to do (cf. Ps 104:4). Created beings give glory to God when they develop the full potential they have been granted. However, we often misuse our freedom and fail to become fully human. At times we even cease to be human. We are free not to know ourselves and not to develop according to the plan of God.

Discussion 2

Doing the truth in love: What masks the truth? Prejudice? Events? Circumstances?

All race prejudice and class prejudice is atheism in practice. Whether we realise it or not, we have to accept what John says in both Gospel and Epistle, that to love God and at the same time hate my sister or brother is impossible.

- What might it mean to be loved and accepted unconditionally by someone?
- Is it possible?
- What would the features of such a love be?

Discussion 3

Recognise and make space for the gift of God, for example, the cave in Francis' life.

> For no one is in any way disposed for divine contemplation that leads to mystical ecstasy unless like Daniel he is a man of desires (Dan 9:23). Such desires are enkindled in us in two ways: by an outcry of prayer that makes us call aloud in the groaning of our hearts and by the flash of insight by which the mind turns most directly, and intently toward the rays of light.[3]

As God gives us freedom, we must give God freedom to be God. In all circumstances, whether individually or collectively, we must leave room for the Spirit to act in a creative way. Only God can give life, only God can be creative; God cannot be manipulated, limited or controlled. Our part is to trust in the power of God, and give God maximum freedom to be and to act. 'You make the wings your messengers, and flaming fire your ministers.' 'How beautiful are all his works, even to the sparse and fleeting vision' (Ps 104:4; 42:23).

- What would it mean for us to give God total freedom in his activity and concern for us?
- How can we make the most of God's freedom so as to act in us?

Discussion 4

Are you somebody?

In her book entitled *Are You Somebody?* Nuala O'Faoláin asks:

> But who am I? Am I the one on television? ... It sometimes happens in the lounge bar, say women at another table, as night goes by start looking at me, or pointing, or in the supermarket someone who has just pushed their trolley past me pulls it back to peer into my face. They think they have seen me before, but they are not quite sure – are you somebody? they frankly ask.[4]

Nuala is now over fifty and lives on her own with her dog and cat. It is only now that she feels ready and fit to be a mother, and a good mother at that. Yes! Experience can teach. Insight and behavioural change go together. All her life prior to that:

I was recreating my mother's life – she sat in her chair in a flat in Dublin and read, and drank. My mother was not interested in friendship, just passion for my father. She didn't value any other relationship. She was the daughter of an ideal couple! It is hard for history to explain that the individual comes out of a vessel into which two jugs called 'heredity' and 'environment' have been poured.[5]

We human beings have our feelings, and they tell us something. However, we rarely know ourselves. We are a mixture. In our lack of self-knowledge we often run the risk of entering the kind of world and relationships that are not for our genuine fulfilment. We then hide behind systems and principles. If the intellect was everything, we would long ago have answered Pilate's question, 'What is truth?' The emotional life is subtle. Very few of us know ourselves, or indeed see ourselves as others see us. If we really accept a Creator God, then only God sees us as we really are, and we should not be afraid of that. In fact, because we are beloved of God, and because we believe that it is out of love that we are named and born, the discovery of who we are and the question 'Are we somebody?' can only find its answer in God.

'What was bitter for me became sweet,' said Francis. Jarring experiences can bring our world-view (vision or theory) into question. However, time spent with God will enable us to see our history as positively making us who we are now, as well as the nature of our destiny, our uniqueness, and our calling. Henri Nouwen expresses it thus:

> Beneath much human assertiveness, competitiveness, and rivalry; beneath much self-confidence and even arrogance, there is often a very insecure heart, much less sure of itself than outward behaviour would lead one to believe. I have

often been shocked to discover that men and women with obvious talents and with many rewards for their accomplishments have so many doubts about their own goodness. Instead of experiencing their outward successes as a sign of their inner beauty, they live them as a cover-up for their sense of personal worthlessness. Not a few have said to me: 'If people only knew what goes on in my innermost self, they would stop with their applause and praise.'

I vividly remember talking with a young man loved and admired by everyone who knew him. He told me how a small critical remark from one of his friends had thrown him into an abyss of depression. As he spoke, tears streamed from his eyes and his body twisted in anguish. He felt that his friend had broken through his wall of defences and had seen him as he really was: an ugly hypocrite, a despicable man beneath his gleaming armour. As I heard this story, I realised what an unhappy life he had lived, even though the people around him had envied him for his gifts. For years he had walked around with the inner questions: 'Does anyone really love me? Does anyone really care?' And every time he had climbed a little higher on the ladder of success, he had thought: 'This is not who I really am; one day everything will come crashing down, and then people will see that I am no good'. This encounter illustrates the way many people live their lives – never fully sure that they are loved as they are. Many have horrendous stories that offer very plausible reasons for their low self-esteem; stories about parents who did not give them what they needed, about teachers who mistreated them, about friends who betrayed them, and about a Church which left them out in the cold during a critical moment of their life.

The parable of the Prodigal Son is a story that speaks about a love that existed before any rejection was possible, and that would still be there after all rejections have taken place. It is the love and everlasting love of a God who is father as well as mother. It is the fountain of all true human love, even the most limited.

It might sound strange, but God wants to find me as much as, if not more than, I want to find God. Yes, God needs me as much as I need God. God is not the patriarch who stays home, doesn't move, and expects his children to come to him, apologise for their aberrant behaviour, beg for forgiveness, and promise to do better. To the contrary, he leaves the house, ignoring his dignity by running towards them, pays no heed to apologies and promises of change, and brings them to the table prepared for them.

…I am beginning now to see how radically the character of my spiritual journey will change when I no longer think of God as hiding and making it as difficult as possible for me to find God but, instead, as the one who is looking for me, while I am doing the hiding. When I look through God's eyes at my lost self and discover God's joy at my coming home, then my life may become less anguished and more trusting.

Can I accept that I am worth looking for? Do I believe that there is a desire in God to simply be with me?

…Here lies the core of my spiritual struggle: the struggle against self-rejection, self-contempt, and self-loathing. It is a very fierce battle because the world and its demons conspire to make me think about myself as worthless, useless, and negligible. Many consumerist economies stay afloat by manipulating the low self-esteem of their consumers, and by creating spiritual expectations through material means. As long as I am kept 'small', I can easily be seduced to buy things, meet people, or go places that promise a radical change in self-concept, even though they are totally incapable of bringing this about. But every time I allow myself to be thus manipulated or seduced, I will have still more reasons for putting myself down and seeing myself as *the unwanted child.*[6]

Are you somebody? Am I somebody? How do people evaluate one another? How do I evaluate myself? What values have I, really, or how would I act in order to be valuable to others, if that is what I wish to be?

We really need to be still, silent, listening, in order to give God the opportunity to reassure and convince us that we always have been and always will be somebody special, unique and cherished. Only then will we discover our world. Only then will we experience true security, true freedom, and our very selfhood. We are often afraid to know who we are and, like Adam and Eve, we hide our nakedness. We hide from God, from truth, from reality.

- Are you somebody?
- Have you allowed God to help you look inside?

Discussion 5
View of self
Do you understand yourself pretty well? Of the following, tick those to which you would answer 'Yes'.

- Do you feel on top of the world when you reach a goal you set?
- Are you often a puzzle to yourself?
- Do you think that God has something to do with who you are right now?
- Would you like to understand yourself better?
- Do you depend on God for direction?
- Do you think that you have to step on someone to get ahead?
- Did you do something this week that you are proud of?
- Do you think you learn more when you go through the struggles of making your own choices?
- Do you think that taking on the consequences of your decisions has disciplined your choices?
- Do you consider yourself a perfectionist?
- Do you give up a hobby because you are not good at it?
- Are you bored by routine?

Discussion 6

Success

Do you think that success:

- is allowing yourself to become the person God intends you to be?
- is the capacity to change?
- is a goal to be reached by age fifty or sixty?
- has already changed for you – you've changed your ideas of what it really means during the last five years?

Do you think that for many people success refers only to material things? Do you feel successful? Have you ever felt successful, yet found that no one recognises your success?

Do you think that success:

• is liking yourself?
• is knowing and standing up for what you believe?
• takes hard work?

> If you can dream – and not make dreams your master,
> If you can think – and not make thoughts your aim,
> If you can meet with Triumph and Disaster
> And treat those two imposters just the same:
> If you can bear to hear the truth you've spoken
> Twisted by knaves to make a trap for fools,
> Or watch the things you gave your life to, broken,
> And stoop and build'em up with worn-out tools…
> Yours is the Earth and everything that's in it,
> And – which is more – you'll be grown up, my child![7]
> (Rudyard Kipling)

Maybe some of the group could enlighten the gathering from their own experiences on the emptiness of fame and the opportunities afforded by failure. Perhaps participants might exchange their personal views of self and allow others to give their view of 'who am I?'

Discussion 7
War, self-revelation

> War is one of many forms of the breaking of the vessels, to use a metaphor from Kabbalistic spirituality. In the Jewish Kabbalah, the fractured nature of human existence came about as the result of the overflowing of divine light into vessels too rigid to contain it: A twentieth century American poet speaks of it, the 'invasion of the over-soul

into a cup too brittle, a jar too circumscribed'. According to tradition, those insufficient vessels shattered into shards and fragments, and their integrity must be restored by arduous spiritual exercise. So too, there is an element in human cataclysm, such as war, which represents not wholly the descent of darkness, but, paradoxically, a spring of light – or perhaps, from the human perspective, an inextricable confluence of light and dark. In other words, catastrophe is itself the evidence of divine presence, with all its ambivalent power.[8]

God is not the author of war. War begins in the human heart. God does not desire war, but God is present everywhere. Jesus Christ descended into the darkest areas of our existence.

We can with God's help create an opportunity for growth from an evil situation.

> The poet powerfully gives the sense of the devastation of war as a divine event, and following her meditation we may grasp something of the character of apocalypse. The conflagrations in sky and earth, the brilliant terror of the exploding bombs, shattered the brittle case, the husk of self. The divine character of the cataclysm does not in her vision represent divine retribution [still the commonest, most pervasive understanding of human catastrophe], but more specifically it signals an 'uncovering,' bringing with it a mysterious sense of revelations, of grace moving within the rubble of lives, of presence within the rubble of buildings.[9]

In drawing attention to war (catastrophe) the poet makes the point that truth is not necessarily revealed solely through ecstatic experiences of comfort and peace. All circumstances and events have the potential of revealing the glory and presence of God to us. God is in control and God is present in all. The Cross can show us the beauty of love.

> Oh, God, my God, hear me also, a widow. It is you who are the author of those events and of what preceded and followed them. The present, also, and the future you have planned. Whatever you devise comes into being. (The prayer of Judith, from Judith 9:5.)

> Any context in which you can be thoroughly comfortable is likely to prove deadening. A seed wrapped in sterilised cotton and sheltered in a vault may lie there a long time, but it will not sprout. Another seed, tossed where it will be chilled by winter before being warmed and wet by spring rains, will be awakened and will yield fruit.[10]

- 'Failure' and 'disaster' can often help people to grow in stature. Can you give examples?
- Mary Craig *(Blessings)* says that we lose ourselves in the process if we run away from our own battles. Viktor Frankl states that it is the 'decisions' we make, not the conditions, that determine whether we grow or develop. In your own life, can you say that decisions you have made were life-giving for you and for others?
- Can faith empower the poor and oppressed in their suffering situations? How?

Discussion 8
Taking ourselves too seriously – the road to penance, to asceticism, to fasting, to the demands of love.

Clare gave similar advice to Agnes of Prague, telling her to refrain from an impossible and indiscreet austerity, saying: '[So act] that living, you may praise the Lord, giving to him your reasonable service, and let your sacrifice always be seasoned with salt'. This seasoning with salt that they both mention is in accordance with the instruction in Leviticus about sacrifice [Lev 2:13], and they understood it to represent that sense of proportion and that pinch of dry humour which stop us taking things too seriously. Our human nature will be slightly comic no matter what we do, and there is much wisdom in peacefully enjoying it, so we can season our serious approach to spirituality with a touch of astringency.[11]

• What do you understand penance to mean? How did Francis/Clare understand it?
• What might penance mean for us today?

Discussion 9
Identity – Who am I?
Because of the emphasis on achievement as success or progress, particularly in our Western culture, it happens that many suffer from anxiety, stress and a feeling of gross inadequacy. They feel they will never make it in the so-called 'rat race'. The reason is that competition seems at times to be at the very heart of reality and survival: 'I must win to succeed, I must win to be recognised, I must win to be first'. However, St Paul's idea of winning the race was winning the struggle within himself to overcome the temptations that threatened to stop him from learning who God was, who Jesus was, who he was himself and what his mission was.

He raced for a prize that was an 'imperishable crown'.
(1 Cor 9:25)

God is the life-giver. God is the prize and Jesus is the trainer and mentor. Paul's emphasis is on the fact that, in ordinary, everyday life, many discipline themselves to achieve a prize that won't last – a 'perishable crown'.

We should realise that the prize of fruitfulness, the imperishable crown, involves discipline as well.

> I do not run aimlessly…. No. I drive my body and train it for fear that after having preached to others I myself should be disqualified. (1 Cor 9:26-27)

Developing faith and trust involves discipline and it needs to be nurtured and trained. Paul says 'I have competed well. I have finished the race. I have kept the faith' (2 Tim 4:7).

Obviously we can be surrounded by an unhealthy competitiveness that may mitigate against our faith and our growth in the knowledge of God and of ourselves.

Nouwen, McNeill and Morrison, in their book entitled *Compassion,* talk about people's fear of losing their identity if they are not competitive in this way:

> This fear, which is very real and influences much of our behaviour, betrays our deepest illusions: that we can forge our own identities; that we are the collective impression of our surroundings, that we are the trophies and distinctions we have won. This, indeed, is one of our greatest illusions. It makes us into competitive people who compulsively cling to our differences and defend them at all costs, even to the point of violence.[12]

Admonition 5:

> Be conscious, O man, of the wondrous state in which the

Lord God has placed you, for He created you and formed you to the image of His beloved Son, according to the body, and to his likeness according to the spirit (cf. Genesis 1:26).[13]

Then, Admonition 1, Verse 16:

See, daily He humbles Himself (cf. Phil 2:8) as when He came from the royal throne (Wis 18:15) into the womb of the Virgin....[14]

The creature is beloved by the Creator to such a degree that the Creator respects and cherishes the physical body, and Christ takes on that body. But not only that, that body is worthy to be his royal throne while he is here. I need to understand that I am beloved and good in both body and spirit. And this is the first fact of life, that God looks at me as good, desires my company, wants to be my friend, and hopes that I will recognise this, particularly in the events of my own life. All that we are, even our limitations, because we are creatures, is cherished by God.

Letter to the Faithful II:

Through his angel, Saint Gabriel, the most high Father in heaven announced this Word of the Father – so worthy, so holy and glorious – in the womb of the most holy and glorious Virgin Mary, from which he received the flesh of humanity and our frailty.[15]

From the Office of the Passion, Psalm II:4:

Since it is You who drew me out of the womb, You, my hope from my mother's breasts, I am cast upon You from the womb (Ps 21:10).[16]

112

Psalm 12:5:

> In You I have been supported from birth; from my
> mother's womb. You are my protector and of You my song
> will always be (Ps 70:6).[17]

From A Letter To The Entire Order:

> 21. Listen, my brothers; If the blessed Virgin is so
> honoured, as it is right, since she carried Him in [her] most
> holy womb; if the blessed Baptist trembled and did not
> dare to touch the holy head of God; if the tomb in which
> He lay for some time is so venerated, how holy, just and
> worthy must be the person who touches [Him] with his
> hands, receives [Him] in his heart and mouth, and offers
> [Him] to others to be received. [This is] He who is now
> not about to die, but Who is eternally victorious and
> glorified, upon Whom the angels desire to gaze (1 Pet
> 1:12).[18]

This again shows the desire of God to give life right from the
very beginning to human beings, to be part of them and to
consider them in their limited state as being worthy of love. As
we consider our own histories, with our limitations and failures,
it is necessary for us to see also that in and through us there
exists a God who loves and who wishes us to see ourselves as
God sees us, in order that we may cherish, respect and love
ourselves.

Again this strong emphasis on ourselves as images of God
should emphasise for us that God is our parent and that Jesus is
a guide, brother and mother to us. Francis used this kind of
imagery: a mother loves her children. Julian of Norwich says
'the Christ mother feeds his children not with milk, but with

himself. He not only shelters his child against harm, but does good against evil, transforming everything in us – our limitations, the wounds of sin – into marks of honour.' Julian directs us not to address Christ as mother but rather to see in him the office, properties and activities of motherhood.[19]

In this first part, it is necessary to consider the reality of the self – the beloved, authentic self. Even the desert fathers practised in order to discover themselves:

> These monks staked everything on the effort to destroy illusion and deception. Their various disciplines were intended to help them cut through the noise of lives hooked on the deceptions, materialisms and games which have characterised human beings since the Fall. The desert itself gave them a landscape, which mirrored what they sought for their own hearts: an uncluttered view through clear air.

> The principal element of that process was offering the secrets of one's heart to another person for discernment. This was typically done by a young, or at any rate, novice, monk to his abba, his monastic elder. This practice of self-revelation was both the means and the fruit of the monk's growth and singleness of heart. This theme is one which is particularly interesting for modern people presumably because it is something we would like to do ourselves but find very difficult.[20]

- To confront does not necessarily mean to bully, frighten or condemn. How might you help somebody face the challenge of the reality of their situation in a loving and life-giving way?

Discussion 10
Discipline to work on the self

Perhaps another way to understand all of this is to remember that it was the commitment to truth, to seeing things as they are, which disposed the monk for contemplation of God. The classic hierarchies of contemplation described by Evagrius and others moved from disciplined work on the self to contemplation of the created world, to contemplation of the spiritual world, to contemplation of God. The commitment to truth is initially expressed and realised in the ascetical labour of self-knowledge. To see things as they are, to see God as God can be seen, without masks of fantasy, projections and pious wishes depends in the first place upon stripping away the masks of fantasies and projections about ourselves. We find that the masks we place on ourselves, the masks we see on the face of God, are, in the end, the same, and are of our own making.

One must remember that the practice is best described as manifestation of thought and not just confession of sins. The dominant values here are humility and obedience rather than penitence and pardon.[21]

John Climacus compared unrevealed thoughts in the heart to eggs placed in warm dung: The thoughts are bound to hatch evil deeds unless revealed.[22]

The ability of a monk freely to open his heart to his abba indicated growth and humility. The revelation breaks the hold of unreality. The desert fathers were absolutely committed to breaking the cycle of deception which began with Adam and Eve... the tragedy of Adam and Eve was that they hid. Far from thinking of themselves like God, they thought of God like themselves, and thinking God could not bear their failure, they hid.[23]

The above quotations from Columba Stewart's *Radical Honesty about the Self* might be useful for reflection. Reflections can be shared. This tradition goes back to the fourth century.

Discussion 11
Concepts and key words that surround humility

Add and subtract words, sentences and key words from the following list that come to mind when we talk about true humility. Bear in mind what Francis loved to say about *minoritas*, about being lesser brethren, poor sisters, the poor Christ.

Humility	Minority	Belonging
Self	Sense of self	Contemplation
My history	My story	Circumstances of my life events
Action of God	Faithfulness to myself	Fidelity
My values	My past	My present
My identity	Accepting myself	My limitations
My relationships	I am the beloved	Mystic
Solitude	Silence	Stillness
Obedience	Providence	Decisions
Who am I?	To see	Reality
Pretence	Prejudice	Awareness of self

Illusion	Aspirations	Desires
Chance	Value to God	Fear
Response	What threatens Me?	There must be a reason

Being loved

Being loved unconditionally

Positive and negative life events

Discussion 12
Self-Acceptance

How much do we accept ourselves as we are? Participants should write down what they dislike in themselves. There is no need to impart this information to anyone else. It is important to appreciate what we really dislike in ourselves, at all levels: physical, emotional, psychological, sexual, intellectual, spiritual. We should then admit what we would like to be at all of those levels.

If offered three of the following ten choices, what would they be in order of preference? With nobody else around, what would I honestly desire at this moment? What are my values? Which of the following are important to me? Rate from one to ten.

1. To win a very large amount of money.
2. Friendship (to have many friends).
3. To possess the ability to love, to be truthful, to forgive.
4. To have success in examinations or in business.
5. To have a 'status' job, recognised as being important.
6. To be understood.
7. To be a celebrity.
8. To be in a position of power.
9. To be poor.
10. To have the capability of being a good friend, faithful and loyal.

Discussion 13
Knowing oneself
'Who do you say I am?' It is always a demanding question, addressed to all lives and that of the entire Church. It permanently tests the Christian faith, leading to its ultimate consequences.[24]

• How do I see myself in relation to God? To Christ?
• Talk this over with God.

Francis' great discovery was that he was somebody of great importance in relation to God. In contrast, in relation to anybody else, the value that he had could be transient and fleeting. Francis discovered among the lepers a quality of sweetness, which he, like Clare, attributed to God's presence. Clare and Francis spoke of a treasure, the 'sweetness' of poverty. They spoke of relationships here on earth that had the savour of heaven and the closeness of blood relationships, i.e. in the language of mother, sister, brother, father.

• Can we discern what reality was in the lives of Francis and Clare?
• In today's world, why do people value money so much?
• What have we got to give?
• Do we think that we have nothing to give particularly if we have neither gold nor silver?

Discussion 14
Friendship
In friendship, gifts of money and goods can be patronising. They can enslave, demean, attempt to force the other to please, to pretend, to be beholden.

- In what way were Francis and Clare able to establish true friendships?
- Does this have any practical implications for personal relationships?
- Do I need to 'buy' friendship in order to belong or to be wanted?
- From what I sometimes read or know of Scripture, are there any sayings or passages that I avoid?

SIGNIFICANT EVENTS IN THE LIFE OF FRANCIS

The sensitivity of both Francis and Clare to God's active word in the Bible meant that they allowed that word to throw light on their experiences. Events and circumstances in their lives thus became a word of God spoken to them.

It is a good idea for the participants to look at the events in Francis' life that gradually helped him to see reality and thus to begin to grow. Some of these events assisted him towards a new vision of reality, which dispelled all illusion for him.

These events include:

- Imprisonment.
- Sickness.
- The vision of arms not related to usual warfare but to spiritual warfare.
- The sojourn at San Damiano.
- The renunciation before the bishop.
- The meeting with the leper.
- Hearing the gospel.
- Period of probation of the Rule.
- Discerning his mission.
- Preaching before the sultan.
- Taming the wolf of Gubbio.
- Receiving the stigmata.

Clare also broke away from the snares of the illusory. We do not have on record much about the aspirations or private thoughts of Clare as a young woman. We do know that her reputation was one of holiness and that she had dedicated herself early in life to the service of God. However, certain events in her life were significant in retrospect.

These events include:

- Palm Sunday, 18 March 1212.
- Staying at convents of the Benedictine Order and the move to San Damiano.
- The conversion of Clare's sister, Agnes.
- The Saracens' flight.
- Her influence on the city of Assisi and her freeing of that city.
- The papal approbation of Clare's unusual Rule.

Reflection 1

Imprisonment in the life of Francis

In the Legend of the Three Companions, Chapter 2:4, it states that during the year of the war between Perugia and Assisi, Francis was captured, together with many of his former fellow citizens, and was taken to prison in Perugia. Because of his distinguished bearing, he was put among the nobles. One day his companions were especially downhearted, but Francis, who was naturally cheerful, seemed almost to be enjoying himself. One of his fellow prisoners reproached him as a fool for looking happy at being in prison. Francis answered: 'Is that what you think of me? The day will come when I shall be honoured by the whole world'.

Among his companions there was one who had injured a fellow prisoner. Because of this all the others ignored him. Francis alone refused to do this and urged them to follow his example. After a year, at the conclusion of the war, he and other prisoners returned to Assisi.[25]

> John prophesied enclosed within the hidden places of his mother's womb; Francis prophesied future events enclosed within the prison of this world while he was still ignorant of the divine counsel. Indeed, once when there was a bloody battle between the citizens of Perugia and those of Assisi, Francis was made captive with several others, and endured the squalors of a prison. His fellow captives were consumed with sorrow, bemoaning miserably their imprisonment; Francis rejoiced in the Lord, laughed at his chains and despised them. His grieving companions resented his happiness and considered him insane and mad. Francis replied prophetically: 'Why do you think I rejoice? There is another consideration, for I will yet be venerated as a saint throughout the whole world.' And so it has truly come about; everything he said has been fulfilled.[26]

> There was at that time among his fellow prisoners a certain proud and completely unbearable knight whom the rest were determined to shun, but Francis' patience was not disturbed. He put up with the unbearable knight and brought the others to peace with him. Capable of every grace, a chosen vessel of virtues, he poured out his gifts on all sides.[27]

Celano and the three companions were writing about a saint, not the Francis who was imprisoned. We can learn far more from prisoners as to what might have been going on in his mind. Only if we listen to those who have experienced imprisonment can we really see the significance of this event and how God speaks to us through such events.

We also see historical events, in our own lives or in the lives of others, through a tinted lens. Often we have a purpose in interpreting an event.

The Amish have a custom, when they are making rugs, of leaving a hole in their work to remind them that life is full of mistakes, for oftentimes it is only through the mistakes that God can enter.

Points to Ponder
- What is hagiography?
- What might be the purpose of a hagiographer in writing?
- How might the hagiographer's approach be conditioned?
- How might his or her lens be tinted?
- What about Thomas of Celano in this respect?
- Have you ever been imprisoned?
- What was it like?
- Do you know anybody who has been imprisoned?

Reflection 2
Francis' sickness

3. That man was still boiling in the sins of youthful heat, and his unstable time of life was driving him without restraint to carry out the laws of youth. At the very time when he, not knowing how to become tame, was aroused by the venom of the ancient serpent, the divine vengeance, or rather the divine anointing, came upon him. This aimed, first of all, at recalling his erring judgement by bringing distress to his mind and affliction to his body, according to that prophecy: Behold I will hedge up your path with thorns, and I will stop it with a wall.

Thus worn down by a long illness, as human obstinacy

deserves since it is rarely remedied except through punishment, he began to mull over with himself things that were not usual for him. When he had recovered a little and, with the support of a cane, had begun to walk about here and there through the house in order to regain his health, he went outside one day and began to gaze upon the surrounding countryside with greater interest. But the beauty of the fields, the delight of the vineyards, and whatever else was beautiful to see could offer him no delight at all. He wondered at the sudden change in himself, and considered those who loved these things quite foolish.

4. From that day he began to regard himself as worthless and to hold in some contempt what he had previously held as admirable and loveable, though not completely or genuinely. For he had not yet been freed from the bonds of vanities nor had he thrown off from his neck the yoke of degrading servitude. It is difficult to leave familiar things behind, and things once instilled in the spirit are not easily weakened. The spirit, even a long time after its early training, reverts to them; and vice, with enough custom and practice, becomes second nature.[28]

Bonaventure, in the Major Legend, wrote:

2. As yet, however, Francis had no idea of God's plan for him. He was completely taken up with the affairs of his father's business, and his mind was intent on the things of earth because of the corruption of human nature, so that he had never learned to raise his mind to heaven, or acquired a taste for the things of God. Adversity is one of the best means of sharpening a person's spiritual

perception and so 'the power of the Lord reached out to him and the Most High relented in His dealings with him' (Ez. 1, 3; Ps 76, 11). God brought him low with a prolonged illness, in order to prepare his soul to receive the Holy Spirit. When he recovered and was going about dressed as usual in keeping with his position, he met a knight of noble birth but very poor, so that he was not properly clad. Francis felt sorry for him and immediately took off his own clothes and gave them to him. At one and the same time he fulfilled the twofold duty of relieving the poverty of the poor and saving a nobleman from embarrassment.[29]

A prolonged illness in anybody's life can make changes. It can lead to depression or to self-knowledge, to a new outlook on life and new hope.

Points to Ponder
- Have there been such incidents in your life?
- How have you responded in the past?
- How do you respond now?

Reflection 3
Francis' vision of arms
According to Celano, Francis tried to forget what he had learned in his sickness:

4. ...Thus Francis still tried to avoid the divine grasp, and, for a brief time losing sight of the Father's reproach while good fortune smiled upon him, reflected upon worldly matters. Ignoring God's plan, he vowed, out of vainglory and vanity, to do great deeds. A certain nobleman from the city of Assisi was furnishing himself on a large scale with

military weaponry and, swollen by the wind of empty glory, he asserted solemnly that he was going to Apulia to enrich himself in money or distinction. When Francis heard of this, because he was whimsical and overly daring, he agreed to go with him. Although Francis did not equal him in nobility of birth, he did outrank him in graciousness; and though poorer in wealth, he was richer in generosity.

5. …One night, after Francis had devoted himself with all his deliberation to accomplish these things and was eager, seething with desire, to make the journey, the One who had struck him with the rod of justice visited him in a vision during the night in the sweetness of grace. Because he was eager for glory, the Lord exalted and enticed him to its pinnacle. For it seemed to him that his whole house was filled with soldiers' arms; saddles, shields, spears and other equipment. Though delighting for the most part, he silently wondered to himself about its meaning. For he was not accustomed to see such things in his house, but rather stacks of cloth to be sold. He was greatly bewildered at the sudden turn of events and the response that all these arms were to be for him and his soldiers. With a happy spirit he awoke the next morning. Considering his vision a prediction of great success, he felt sure that his upcoming journey to Apulia would be successful. In fact he did not know what he was saying and as yet he did not at all understand the gift sent to him from heaven. He should have been able to see some semblance of great deeds, his spirit was not moved by these things in its usual way. In fact, he had to force himself to carry out his plans and undertake the journey he had desired.

It is a fine thing
that at the outset mention be made of arms,
and very fitting
that arms be handed over
to a soldier about to do battle
with one strong and fully armed.
Thus,
like a second David
in the name of the Lord God of hosts
from the long-standing abuse of its enemies,
he might liberate Israel.[30]

6. ...Changed in mind but not in body, he now refused to go to Apulia and was anxious to direct his will to God's. Thus he retired for a short time from the tumult and business of the world and was anxious to keep Jesus Christ in his inmost self. Like an experienced merchant, he concealed the pearl he had found from the eyes of mockers and selling all he had, he tried to buy it secretly.

Now there was in the city of Assisi a man he loved more than all the rest. They were of the same age and the constant intimacy of their mutual love made him bold to share his secrets with him. He often brought him to remote places suitable for talking, asserting that he had found a great and valuable treasure.[31]

At this stage, Celano says that Francis went into a certain grotto and thought about the treasure that he had found and what he was going to do, and at the same time reflected. However, when he came out of the grotto, he said that he did not want to go to Apulia, but he promised that he would do noble and great things in his native place. People thought he wished to take to himself a wife, and they asked him, 'Do you want to get married, Francis?' He replied, 'I will take a bride more noble and more beautiful than you have ever seen, and she will surpass the rest in beauty and excel all others in wisdom.'[32]

So often, we ourselves tend to go on a journey or take a direction with tremendous ambition and belief in our own ability. Circumstances may point out to us the folly of our journey, or the possibility that we cannot make it. The truth is that it can be providential for us to take a different direction. Celano, of course, looking back, sees Providence at work and does not outline for us the struggle, the growing self-awareness that was happening within Francis, of who he was, what he could do, his own limitations, aspirations, the passing things of this world – the usual wondering and pondering that always occurs in people who are growing and genuinely want to know what direction they should take.

In the Legend of the Three Companions, again he sees the vision of the beautiful palace and the armour of the warriors, and the answer came to him that these arms were for him and his knights. On awakening, Francis rose

> 5. ...gleefully, thinking, after the manner of worldlings (for he had not yet tasted the spirit of God) that he was destined to become a magnificent prince and that the vision was prophetic of great prosperity. What he had seen spurred him to start for Apulia, and to get himself knighted in the following of Count Gentile. His glee was such that people in surprise asked the reason for his delight, and received the answer, 'I know that I shall become a great prince.'
>
> 6. ...immediately preceding this vision Francis had shown sure signs of nobility and chivalry, for he had given all his

own fine accoutrements and clothes to a poor, needy knight. And we think that this magnanimity played no small part in bringing about the vision.

Now it happened that, after the start for Apulia, Francis felt unwell on arriving at Spoleto; and thinking with apprehension about the journey, he went to bed; but, half asleep, he heard a voice calling and asking him whither he was bound. He replied, telling of his plan. Then he, who had previously appeared to him in sleep, spoke these words:

'Who do you think can best reward you, the Master or the servant?' 'The Master,' answered Francis. 'Then why do you leave the Master for the servant, the rich Lord for the poor man?' Francis replied: 'Oh, Lord, what do you wish me to do?' 'Return to your own place' he was bidden, 'and you will be told what to do. You must interpret your vision in a different sense. The arms and palace you saw are intended for other knights than those you had in mind, and your principality too will be of another order.' Francis awoke and began to turn all this over in his mind. After the first vision he had been in a transport of delight, filled with desires for worldly prosperity; but this one left him puzzled and perplexed. He thought about it so intensely that he slept no more that night. Immediately at daybreak, he started back towards Assisi in glad expectation that God, who had shown him the vision, would soon reveal his will for the future. Francis now waited to be guided by him for the salvation of his soul. His mind was changed and he gave up all thought of going to Apulia.[33]

We can imagine the return, as it was not the kind of worldly glory that Francis would have desired or expected at the time. Also, as is so often the case, it is in looking back that we see

God's hand, but at the time, the experience is filled with perplexity, with great doubts, because it is 'the narrow way'.

Bonaventure talks of Francis again, and the vision. He says of Francis:

> 3. ...He had no experience of interpreting God's secret revelations and he could not penetrate beyond the appearance of what he saw, to the truth which he could not see, and so when he awoke in the morning he took his extraordinary vision to mean that he was going to achieve great success. He was still ignorant of God's plan for him and he prepared to enlist with a high-ranking knight in Apulia, in the hope of acquiring distinction as a soldier in his service, as his vision seemed to indicate.
>
> He set out shortly afterwards but when he reached the next town, he heard God calling him by his first name as he lay asleep, and saying, 'Francis, who can do more for you, a lord or his servant, a rich man or a beggar?' When he replied that a lord or a rich man could do more, he was asked, 'Then why are you abandoning the Lord to devote yourself to a servant? Why are you choosing a beggar instead of God, who is infinitely rich?' 'Lord,' replied Francis, 'what will you have me do?' And God told him, 'Go back to your own town. The vision which you saw foretold a spiritual achievement which will be accomplished in you by God's will, not man's.' In the morning Francis went back to Assisi without delay. He was overjoyed and had no care for the future; he was already a model of obedience and he waited patiently on God's will.[34]

Bonaventure, in the light of history, sees that Francis' failures indeed were the road to his success, and that it was Francis' acceptance of reality, and eventually his understanding of the Creator, that opened for him the path towards fulfilment.

Points to Ponder

- Looking back on our lives, do we now have a different understanding of our past?
- Can 'failures' still be of benefit to us?
- Can we bring them to God, to the Creator?

Reflection 4
Sojourn at San Damiano

Francis and his companions, so the legends say, after this particular homecoming from Apulia, went frequently to a cave near Assisi,

> 12. …and while the friend, on the lookout for treasure, remained outside, Francis went in alone, and, with his heart full of a new, unaccustomed fervour, he prayed to God his Father. He wished that none should know what he did in the cave but God alone, to whom he prayed assiduously to show him how to find the heavenly treasure.[35]

> 13. …while he was walking near the church of San Damiano, an inner voice bade him go in and pray. He obeyed, and kneeling before an image of the crucified Saviour, he began to pray most devoutly. A tender, compassionate voice then spoke to him: 'Francis, do you not see that my house is falling into ruin? Go, and repair it for me.' Trembling and amazed Francis replied: 'Gladly I will do so, O Lord.' He had understood that the Lord was speaking of that very church which, on account of its age, was indeed falling into ruin.

These words filled him with the greatest joy and inner light because in spirit he knew that it was indeed Jesus Christ who had spoken to him. On leaving the church he found the priest who had charge of it sitting outside, and taking a handful of money from his purse, he said: 'I beg you, Sir, to buy oil and keep the lamp before this image of Christ constantly alight. When this is spent I will give you as much as you need.'

14. From that hour his heart was stricken and wounded with melting love and compassion for the passion of Christ; and for the rest of his life he carried in it the wounds of the Lord Jesus.[36]

The Gospel of John was what Francis chose to imitate very clearly and to have recited to him at his death. It depicts the glorified Jesus, and yet the glory of the suffering Jesus. It is not easy for us to see that the way of love is a way that makes demands, that has its own cost. Francis was to learn and then imitate the self-emptying love of the Incarnation. It meant accepting the pain of loss, of risk, of trust, of being misunderstood, the pain of loyalty, of fidelity and finally of being killed. Francis, like Jesus, absorbed all these in order to bring life, hope, fellowship, fraternity and joy, and thus negate those negative forces. It was this acceptance of suffering with the glory that brought Francis to a new understanding of what it was to rebuild the Church.

Points to Ponder
- How does the life and passion of Jesus speak to me personally in the events of my life?
- Am I prepared to 'let go' in order to see more clearly, hear more clearly?

Reflection 5

The renunciation before the bishop

While Francis may have been vain, ostentatious and ambitious as a young person, he also showed signs of generosity. His father probably saw this as a positive trait, and certainly favoured Francis from the beginning as his heir apparent in every sense of the word. Francis' father was a very successful merchant and Francis had a similar flair and personality suited to the business. Yet he gave up a life of wealth and ease for what he truly believed in, even though this meant alienating his father.

We too must make decisions. We cannot blame conditions; it is decisions that will make or break life for us. We are on our own, and each one of us must take responsibility for our own decisions. When we do this we may often feel isolated, yet this is the price of growth, the price of being able to make one's own decisions in integrity, freedom and love. We will never be able to please everybody; in fact, to please everybody is to be a failure. To be able to make decisions freely means to be able to stand alone, to stand freely, but also, sometimes, to become the object of rejection and misunderstanding. Francis was to experience this way as the way of suffering, the way of glory and, ultimately, the way of the Cross.

Points to Ponder

- How capable am I of making my own decisions?
- Am I guided by the opinions of others?
- Are my decisions those of my parents or peer group, or are they my own?
- Is it true that they may never be my own decisions?
- What about blame, or being subjected to shame?
- Do you consider that Francis broke the fourth commandment by what he did?

- Every person is called to be, in their own right, father and mother. Discuss.

Reflection 6
Our values
In order to understand Francis' decisions and the new values that he embraced, it might be helpful to look at our own value systems.

Leisure
Do you:
- set aside a special time each week for leisure activities you enjoy?
- think everyone needs free time?
- think that Christians should observe the Sabbath by resting from work?
- advocate a four-day work week?
- feel you would take a salary cut for a shorter work week?
- feel that leisure time is a luxury for the rich?
- think that one needs to discipline the use of free time?
- prefer to spend most of your leisure time by yourself or with others?
- feel that having a hobby or a special interest would encourage you to use more leisure time?
- feel that leisure time implies neglect in other areas?

Work
Do you:
- like your job?
- work long hours?
- feel that you are hooked on work?
- get more enjoyment from your job than from your leisure time?

- find your work interfering with your personal life?
- sometimes get frustrated with too much free time?

Outlook on life

Which of the following qualities are the most important to you?
- living responsibly
- being insightful
- being well liked
- being physically attractive
- doing well in a chosen job
- having a good social life
- feeling good about yourself
- being of service to others
- having good personal relationships

Which role is most important to you in life?
- being a good spouse
- being a good parent
- being a whole person
- being a good friend
- being a good daughter or son

Which gives you most satisfaction?
- high marks
- learning something new
- solving a problem

Which of the following is the most important to you?
- status
- money
- comfort

What does this say about you? If you feel there is someone in whom you can confide, show him or her your replies and find out how he or she perceives you.

Reflection 7
The meeting with the leper
In the case of the meeting of Francis with the leper, the various authors who mentioned it write it up as a very dramatic, miraculous event in which the leper is almost Christ in person. The earliest account of Francis meeting a leper occurs in Celano's *First Life of St Francis*. (Celano wrote this between 1228 and 1229.) All of the early writers speak of this incident as almost miraculous. However, it was their way of trying to describe the actions of someone they believed was a saint, one who could transcend what is human, when in fact he was transcending what is dysfunctional in human beings. We are usually unaware that a saint transcends the limitations of prejudices, race or religion in order to reach out. In so transcending, he or she shows us, our own enslavement. For that reason, the early Franciscans, looking back at the first companions of Francis, found it difficult to accept that indeed Francis' desire, and the reality for the early novitiates, was to work among and almost to become lepers. It is very sobering to dwell on the position of lepers in society at that time. Celano's earliest account describes Francis' attitude:

> 17. Then the holy lover of profound humility moved to the lepers and lived with them. For God's sake he served all of them with great love. He washed all the filth from them, and even cleaned out the pus of their sores, just as he said in his Testament: 'When I was in sin, it seemed bitter for me to see lepers, and the Lord himself led me among them and I practised mercy to them.' For he used to say that the sight of lepers was so bitter to him that in the days of his

vanity when he saw their houses even two miles away, he would cover his nose with his hands.

When he started thinking of holy and useful matters with the grace and strength of the Most High, while still in the clothes of the world, he met a leper one day. Made stronger than himself, he came up and kissed him. He then began to consider himself less and less, until by the mercy of the Redeemer, he came to complete victory over himself.[37]

Subsequent hagiographers describe Francis' meeting with the leper as meeting Christ. However, in meeting the leper, he met a person in all the foulness of disease, flaws and degradation, which was the reality of the leper. The leper reminded Francis of the Incarnation, a God who became human, limited and powerless. Therefore Francis could rejoice in embracing the leper because the more he embraced the suffering and rejected person, the more he embraced the God who became human.

Points to Ponder
- Why do I react negatively to some places, people, things in my life?
- What am I avoiding in myself that I need to embrace?

Reflection 8
Hearing the Gospel
Celano writes about Francis going to a place near the city of Assisi, San Damiano, where he began to rebuild a dilapidated and ruined church.

21. ...From there he moved to another place, which is called the 'Portiuncula', where there stood a church of the Blessed Virgin Mother of God that had been built in

ancient times. At that time it was deserted and no one was taking care of it. When the holy man of God saw it so ruined, he was moved by piety because he had a warm devotion to the Mother of all good and he began to stay there continually. The restoration of that church took place in the third year of his conversion. At this time he wore a sort of hermit's habit with a leather belt. He carried a staff in his hand and wore shoes.

22. One day the gospel was being read in that church about how the Lord sent out his disciples to preach. The holy man of God, who was attending there, in order to understand better the words of the gospel, humbly begged the priest after celebrating the solemnities of the Mass to explain the gospel to him. The priest explained it all to him thoroughly line by line. When he heard that Christ's disciples should not possess gold or silver or money, or carry on their journey a wallet or a sack, nor bread nor a staff, nor to have shoes nor two tunics, but that they should preach the kingdom of God and penance, the holy man, Francis, immediately exulted in the spirit of God. 'This is what I want', he said, 'this is what I seek, this is what I desire with all my heart.' The holy father, *overflowing with joy*, hastened to implement the words of salvation, and did not delay before he devoutly began to put into effect what he heard. Immediately, he took off the shoes from his feet, put down the staff from his hands, and, satisfied with one tunic, exchanged his leather belt for a cord.[38]

Francis did not seek a fundamental understanding of the Gospel. He sought the spirit of the Gospel and it allowed God to speak to him. He was intent on walking in the footsteps of

Christ – the human face of God, the Creator. He entered into the events of Christ's life with a passion, knowing that the tradition of the Gospels handed on to him would open the mystery of God, made man in Jesus, for him. In his grasp of the story of the Birth, Incarnation and Passion of Jesus, he intuitively grasped the poverty and helplessness of God. He saw that the Incarnation meant a God divested of all power, save that of love.

Points to Ponder

- Have I allowed the word of God to come alive for me?
- With the help of others (in discussion), have I tried to discover what the Gospel might be saying to me now? Is the word of God active and alive?
- Can I create a situation with others whereby the word of God might become active and alive for us now?

Reflection 9

Period of Probation of the Rule

People wanted to follow and imitate Francis' lifestyle, something he never really anticipated or intended. This brought the necessity for a Rule of life for this growing community. Bernard and Peter were among the first to come to Francis.

> 27. Bernard… well knew how luxuriously Francis had lived in the world, therefore, when he saw how he laboured to restore ruined churches and what a harsh life he led, Bernard too resolved to sell his possessions.

And equally,

> 28. …Peter, who also wished to join them, they went to the church of Saint Nicholas near the chief square of the

city. They went in to pray, but, being simple men, they did not know how to find the passage of the Gospel telling of the renunciation of the world. Therefore, they besought God that he would show them his will the first time they opened the book.

29. When their prayer was ended, blessed Francis, kneeling before the altar, took the closed book, opened it and saw written: 'If you wish to be perfect, sell what you have, and give to the poor, and you shall have treasure in heaven' (Mt 19, 21). At this, blessed Francis gave thanks to God with great joy; but because of his devotion to the blessed Trinity, he desired a threefold confirmation of the words and opened the book of the Gospel a second and third time. At the second opening he read: 'Take nothing for your journey' (Lk 9, 3), and at the third: 'If any man will come after me, let him deny himself'(Mt 16, 24).[39]

It is obvious that Francis wanted to give God space, and he recognised that it is difficult sometimes for people, with all their motivations, to really discern what God's will is. The Legend of the Three Companions, in which this event is recorded, is referring to a *sortes apostolorum*, which was frowned on by the Church, as it might have been construed as almost manipulating God. Yet it shows that Francis was a simple man of God, a layman, and his one desire was to know God's will. He would have found it very difficult to know what to do, in particular with respect to those followers. Again, in Celano's second Life, we find Francis worried at the thought of even trying to get a Rule approved for this group. Francis would have been well aware of the heretical groups around him, groups of people that were condemned by the Church, and he had a dream:

209. ...It seemed to him that he had to gather the finest crumbs of bread from the ground and to distribute them to the many hungry brothers who were standing around him. But while he was afraid to distribute such small crumbs lest such minute particles of dust should fall from his hands, a voice spoke to him from above: 'Francis, make one host out of all these crumbs and give it to those who want to eat it.' When he did this, those who did not receive devoutly, or who despised the gift they had received, were soon seen to be greatly infected with leprosy. The saint told all these things to his companions in the morning, regretting that he did not understand the mystery of the vision. But after a little while, while he continued to keep watch in prayer, this voice came down to him from heaven: 'Francis,' it said, 'the crumbs of last night are the words of the Gospel, the host is the rule, the leprosy is wickedness.'[40]

The Rule that Francis was obliged to draw up, since he was attracting followers, had to be referred to Rome for approval. The Fourth Lateran Council had a limitation on the number of Rules that would be allowed. Nevertheless, Francis' primitive Rule was approved by Innocent III. Francis trusted that Providence was at work in all kinds of people, and saw too that the Church itself, despite its blemishes, was a sign for him of approval from God.

Points to Ponder
- Do I wish to 'read the signs of the times' on my own or with others?
- Can we contemplate God in the knowledge of his companionship?
- Can we read more into what is happening in our lives and in the people around us?

- Can we see from the people who are part of our lives how we might know who we are and what our calling is?

Reflection 10
Discerning Francis' mission

Francis considered his vocation to be one of the Lesser Brothers in the world, the *minores*, the *minoritas*. He was convinced that the brothers were called, not only for their own salvation, but for that of many. In the Legend of the Three Companions, St Francis says,

> 36. ...and to this end we are to go through this world exhorting all men and women by our example as well as by our words to do penance for their sins, and to live keeping in mind the commandments of God.[41]

They were to be servants of all, and they were to go out in the manner of the Apostles, following the poor Christ, and taking their identity and any evaluation of them from their relationship with God in Jesus Christ. They were to go out to all peoples. So, in discerning his mission, Francis knew he had to come closer to Christ, whose mission he would be proclaiming. Those co-operating with him in this mission would therefore be the Lesser Brothers, in the manner of Jesus, who washed the feet of his disciples.

Points to Ponder
- Do I aspire to greatness?
- Can I accept that to serve is to be free; it is also to know the dignity of each human being, including myself?

Reflection 11
Preaching before the sultan

Francis' order grew rapidly, so much so that there was a deletion of the existing clergy. The French prelate, Jacques de Vitry, who was earlier very well disposed to Francis, did not like the idea of the loss of any co-workers. He expressed fears at the ease with which the Friars Minor accepted people as friars and then sent them out two by two. However, particularly when Francis was in the 'East', his observations about Francis reveal the impact Francis and his way of life had on people:

> Their master, the founder of the order, came to our army fired with the zeal of faith. He is not afraid to pass over to the enemy's army. He preached the word of God to the Saracens for several days without great result. However, the Sultan, the King of Egypt, asked him in private to beseech the Lord in his name, that he might be divinely inspired to be able to cling to the religion that pleased God the most.[42]

Jacques de Vitry conveys something of Francis' total, deep and firm attitude of peace:

> From the French prelate's words emerge with unmistakable clarity the fact that Francis did not desire to receive any armed protection or safe conduct. In the midst of all-out military action, he moved only by the ardour of his faith and by his missionary spirit.[43]

> Even the Muslims were his brothers, and it was necessary to show them the true way to salvation, which only Jesus Christ could give. In any case, it is hard to understand how he managed to reach the presence of Malek al-Kalil. We get no help from Jordan of Giano when in his Chroniclia, he

says something about Francis' having shouted, 'Sultan! Sultan! until he succeeded in being led to him. That he really was there and did indeed speak to him is beyond doubt. Further proof of this was first pointed out by Louis Massignon, and recently confirmed by Francesco Gabriel. It is possible to find a specific record of this presence of the saint in the biography of an Eqyptian theologian and jurist, Fakhr ad-din al-Farisi. In those years he was very elderly, but also renowned as the spiritual director and counsellor of al-Kamil. In his biography is a record of the conversation that a wise man is said to have had with a Christian monk in the presence of the sovereign. The circumstances were such that they undoubtedly refer only to Francis. Jacques portrays him as passing through the lines apparently during hostilities rather than during a truce, as some have supposed. Jacques wrote after all that Francis 'was not afraid to pass over to the enemy's army'. In any event Malek al-Kamil did him no harm. As was evident in his relations with Frederick II of Swabia, he had an open mind that was attentive to matters of the spirit. He was an enemy of Christians on a political level more than on a cultural or a religious level. Subsequent proof of this was his respect for the truce of over ten years that he established with the Swabian emperor. It was never shaken by any serious incidents.[44]

Bonaventure, as minister general, passed on to the authors of the thirteenth-century *Testimonies* some information about this too. Here are some anecdotes of Brother Illuminato, who accompanied St Francis on his visit to the sultan of Egypt:

13. ...One day the sultan wanted to test the faith and fervour that Blessed Francis manifested towards our

crucified Lord. He had a beautiful multicoloured carpet spread out on the ground; it was almost entirely decorated with motifs in the form of crosses. He said to his spectators: 'Fetch that man who seems to be a true Christian; if in coming towards me he walks on the crosses of the carpet, we will say to him that he insults his Lord. If he refuses to walk on the crosses, I shall ask him why he disdains to approach me.' The man full of God was called. Now, this man received his instructions for his actions as well as for his words from the very plenitude of God. He walked across the carpet from one end to the other and came near the sultan. Then the sultan, thinking that he had found a good opportunity to charge the man of God with having insulted Christ, said to him: 'You Christians adore the cross as a special sign of your God: why then did you not fear to trample underfoot those crosses woven into the rug?' Blessed Francis answered him: 'Thieves were also crucified along with our Lord. We have the true Cross of the Lord and Saviour Jesus Christ; we adore it and show it great devotion; if the holy Cross of the Lord has been given to us, the cross of the thieves has been left to you as your share. That is why I had no scruple in walking over the symbols of brigands....'

The same sultan submitted this problem to him: 'Your Lord taught in his gospels that evil must not be repaid with evil, that you should not refuse your cloak to anyone who wants to take your tunic, etc. (Mt 5:40): in that case, Christians should not invade our land?' 'It seems,' blessed Francis answered, 'that you have not read the gospel of our Lord Jesus Christ completely. In another place we read: 'if your eye causes you to sin, tear it out and throw it away (Mt 5:29). Here he wanted to teach us that every man, however dear and close he is to us, and even if he is as precious to us as the apple of our eye, must be repulsed, pulled out, expelled if he seeks to turn us aside from the faith and love of our God. That is why it is just that Christians invade the land you inhabit, for you blaspheme the name of Christ and alienate everyone you can from his worship. But if you were to recognise, confess, and adore the Creator and Redeemer, Christians would love you as themselves.... All the spectators were in admiration at his answers.[45]

Because to Francis all peoples existed in and through the love of God, he could reach out to the sultan. It was this love of the Creator, the power of the Creator, that Francis recognised in others. He had let go of prejudices and all pretence and thus had grasped the reality of who people were, with their common fears, their defensiveness, and consequently their violence.

Francis, in facing up to reality, accepted all the risks and misunderstandings that this entailed, as was evident when he turned back from riding out to war, suffered loss of face, spurned the tempting values of his father and incurred the ridicule of his townsfolk.

The martyrdom that he was willing to undergo and that he knowingly embraced by turning his back on an affluent and secure lifestyle, was for the sake of spreading the meaning of the life of the suffering, poor Jesus.

Francis went to the sultan in an effort to bring about peace between the two warring factions, Muslims and Christians. In that very moment when he acknowledged the sultan as a brother, each recognised that they had a common Father in heaven. They knew they were related. They knew their true identity in God.

Points to Ponder

- Do I think my God is better than the God of others?
- Am I prepared to see God mirrored to me in other people, other cultures, other religions?
- Can my God be universal? Thomas Merton believed that being Catholic meant being inclusive. Therefore, to the Buddhist he was a Buddhist, to the Hindu, he was a Hindu, in terms of empathy, respect and understanding.

How many of these statements do you agree with?

- We do not learn from other faiths because we generally ignore them or actively reject them.
- Good people of non-Christian faiths are often more virtuous than Christians.
- Persons of the Christian faith generally listen carefully to the ideas of persons of other faiths.
- We can learn much from other groups and other cultures, but people in our Church seldom take the opportunity to do so.
- Most Christians would feel uncomfortable having a Buddhist in their home.
- Doctrine divides, and that is why different denominations have trouble working closely together.
- The ecumenical movement can be destructive if it is carried too far.
- Non-Christians will not have eternal life with God.
- It doesn't matter so much what you believe, as long as you believe in some kind of God.
- Different faiths are just different means to the same end.
- Christians should not try to convert those who believe differently.
- If all religions are seen as equally valid, the real meaning of the Christian faith is diminished.

- First-century traditions are not important to Christians today.
- Christians need continually to examine and re-examine their faith in the light of other world-views.
- Both ancient and modern ideas are needed to understand fully and strengthen one's Christian faith.
- Modern science conflicts with the Christian world-view.
- Evolution and the biblical account of Creation are compatible.
- Most Christians have not closely examined the relationship of the Jewish Passover to the Lord's Supper.

Which of the following would help you most in learning the meaning of faith?
- Exploring the way the Bible defines faith.
- Listening to a theologian talk about faith.
- Putting yourself in Jesus' hands in a risky situation.
- Listening to experiences of others who have lived in faith.

Faith in Jesus is most like which of these?
- A loving relationship with another person.
- Knowing your parents will help you if you ask.
- Trusting from day to day.
- Knowing water will come out of the tap when you turn it on.

Which statement is most important in relating to God?
- Doubts are acceptable; God understands them.
- Faith becomes even stronger when it is tested through doubt.
- We should never doubt.

Our salvation depends upon:
- God's action.
- Our own works.
- Making a decision for Christ.
- Fate – it's already decided who will be saved.

Reflection 12
The taming of the Wolf of Gubbio

This account is in the *Little Flowers of St Francis*. Whether or not we accept some of these stories as true, they can bring home to us some aspect of St Francis that can help us today.

> At a time when St Francis was staying in the town of Gubbio… there appeared in the territory of that city a fearfully large and fierce wolf which was so rabid with hunger that it devoured not only animals but even human beings. All the people in the town considered it such a great scourge and terror – because it often came near the town – that they took weapons with them when they went into the country, as if they were going to war. But even with their weapons they were not able to escape the sharp teeth and raging hunger of the wolf when they were so unfortunate as to meet it….[46]

> …for while the Saint was there at that time, he had pity on the people and decided to go out and meet the wolf.

Of course, the people tried to persuade him not to. But St Francis

> …placed his hope in the Lord Jesus Christ who was master of all creatures. Protected not by a shield or a helmet, but arming himself with the Sign of the Cross, he bravely went

out of the town with his companion, putting all his faith in the Lord who makes those who believe in Him walk without any injury on an asp and a basilisk and trample not merely on a wolf but even on a lion and a dragon....

Some peasants accompanied him a little way... but didn't want to go further. They said, '...that wolf is fierce and we might get hurt.'

When he heard them say this, St Francis answered: 'Just stay here. But I am going on to where the wolf lives.' ...the fierce wolf came running with its mouth open toward St Francis and his companion. The Saint made the Sign of the Cross toward it. And the power of God, proceeding as much from himself as from his companion, checked the wolf and made it slow down and close its cruel mouth.

Then, calling to it, St Francis said: 'Come to me, Brother Wolf. In the name of Christ, I order you not to hurt me or anyone.'

It is marvellous to relate that as soon as he had made the Sign of the Cross, the wolf closed its terrible jaws and stopped running, and as soon as he gave it that order, it lowered its head and lay down at the Saint's feet, as though it had become a lamb.

And St Francis said to it as it lay down in front of him: 'Brother Wolf, you have done great harm in this region, and you have committed horrible crimes by destroying God's creatures without any mercy. You have been destroying not only irrational animals, but you even have the more detestable brazenness to kill and devour human beings made in the image of God. You therefore deserve to be put to death just like the worst robber and murderer. Consequently, everyone is right in crying out against you and complaining, and this whole town is your enemy. But, Brother Wolf, I want to make peace between you and them, so that they will not be harmed by you any more, and after they have forgiven you all your past crimes, neither men or dogs will pursue you any more.'

The wolf showed by moving its body and tail and ears and by a sign of its head that it willingly accepted what the Saint had said and would observe it.

So St Francis spoke again: 'Brother Wolf, since you are willing to make and keep this peace pact, I promise you that I will have the people of this town give you food every day as long as you live, so that you will never again suffer from hunger, for I know that whatever evil you have been doing was done because of the urge of hunger. But my Brother Wolf, since I am obtaining such a favour for you, I want you to promise me that you will never hurt any animal or man. Will you promise me that?'

The wolf gave a clear sign, by nodding its head, that it promised to do what the Saint asked. And St Francis said: 'Brother Wolf, I want you to give me a pledge so that I can confidently believe what you promise.'

And as St Francis held out his hand to receive the pledge, the wolf also raised its front paw and meekly and gently put it in St Francis' hand as a sign that it was giving its pledge.

Then St Francis said: 'Brother Wolf, I order you, in the name of the Lord Jesus Christ, to come with me now, without fear, into the town to make this peace pact in the name of the Lord.'

And the wolf immediately began to walk along beside St Francis, just like a very gentle lamb. When the people saw this, they were greatly amazed, and the news spread quickly throughout the whole town, so that all of them, men as well as women, great and small, assembled in the market place, because St Francis was there with the wolf.[47]

In this story, fear was driving the people to such lengths that they were arming themselves. So often, fear between animals and human beings causes suspicion, greed, defensiveness and conflict. This story brings home what reconciliation means, the taming of the wolf within us, the laying down of arms, and thereby abating the fear that is within all of us.

Chesterton said that the atom bomb in the hands of a Francis of Assisi would be harmless. It is not the scud missile that kills people, rather it is the human heart from which evil springs that kills.

Points to Ponder

• Where does disarmament begin?
• Do we appreciate the wolf within us that is constantly on the defensive – therefore forever attacking?
• Do we recognise it in others?
• Can we tame it by first facing it?
• What am I defending, or why do I act defensively?
• What are my fears? Do I know them? Do I care to know them? If not, are they buried and more dangerous than I really would wish to admit?

Reflection 13
Francis' receiving of the stigmata
St Francis, near the end of his life, had a mystical experience on the Mount of La Verna, a mountain given to him as a gift, in which he was visited by a crucified man appearing as a seraph. He was left with the marks of the crucified Christ after this experience. At the time, there were doubts about these wounds, but it was declared by Gregory IX that, indeed, Francis had received the stigmata, the first person known to do so.

Joanne Schatzein and Daniel Sulmasy, both Franciscan medical experts, in a paper on the illness of Francis, raise the possibility that Francis' wounds stemmed from a leprosy that he had contracted internally, a very painful kind of disease.

This would not in any way reduce the significance of what Francis manifested, because it shows that throughout his life, as he embraced the leper and possibly became one of them, so also did he become one with Christ. Francis was in awe of the whole mystery of the Incarnation: God becoming human, becoming limited, powerless, suffering and identifying with humankind.

Jesus became human, thereby emptying himself. Francis let go of everything, including his health, in order to love, in imitation of Jesus. Francis let go of all possessions and opened wide his hands, to let them be there at the service of all. Francis became one with Christ in an unprecedented way.

The parchment that Francis gave to Brother Leo of Assisi in September 1224 is the first record of the stigmata. It contains the praises of God on one side and a blessing given to Brother Leo on the other. It also contains notes written by Leo in which he says that Francis wrote on the parchment in his own hand while on La Verna two years before his death:

> After the vision and words of the seraph, and the impression of the Stigmata of Christ on his body, he composed these praises written on the other side of the sheet and wrote them in his own hand, giving thanks to God for the kindness bestowed on him.[48]

Leo was the first person to use the Greek word stigma in the way he does. Francis was the first stigmatist in the Church. No word existed to describe Francis' condition. So if Leo did not coin that usage himself, he reflected its new usage within the early Franciscan community. It relates to Paul's, 'I carry the marks (stigmata) of Jesus branded on my body' (Gal 6:17). Of course, Paul was referring to marks or scars from illness, or floggings and stonings. When Francis records his 'thanks to God for the kindness bestowed on him', he could be referring to that mystical experience on La Verna because he had already almost reached his goal to have become as Christ, and Christ had embraced him. This was true reconciliation with Jesus.

Reflection 14
Will of God and life events
Celano, referring to the fact of Francis' physical suffering and death, and his letting go of everything so as to be the obedient servant, fully trusting in God, says:

> 92. …Then he prostrated himself with his heart as much as his body in prayer to God, asking in humble prayer that God in His kindness – the Father of mercies and the God of all consolation – be pleased to show him His will. He prayed earnestly that at the first opening of the book he would be shown what was best for him to do, so that he could bring to complete fulfilment what he had earlier simply and devotedly begun.[49]

> When Francis prayed in the woods and in solitary places, he would fill the woods with sighs, water the places with his tears, strike his breast with his hand.[50]

It has been said of Francis by his biographers that he used to pray with his body as well as his soul. His prayer was often accompanied and sustained by fasting. So he prayed as Jesus prayed to the Father. He prayed inaudibly with his body, and with all that he was. It is no wonder, therefore, that having aligned himself in prayer with Jesus, his body should bear the marks and imprints that Jesus' body bore.

As he welcomed 'Sister Death', St Francis requested that he

hear once again the passage from John's Gospel. He wanted his brothers to read to him the drama that begins with the words 'Before the feast of the Passover... Jesus, knowing that his hour had come to pass from this world to the Father ...' This reading could have included Chapters 13 and 17 of the fourth Gospel, which recounts the washing of the feet and the prayer of Jesus for his disciples. Equally, in Chapter 23 of *The Earlier Rule*, we find that Francis asked Christ, the Holy Spirit and all the saints for help, to thank God for all of creation:

> Because of Your love, we humbly beg... Blessed John the Baptist, John the Evangelist, Peter, Paul, the blessed patriarchs and prophets, the innocents, evangelists, apostles, disciples, martyrs, confessors and virgins, the blessed Elijah and Henoch, all the saints who were, who will be and who are to give You thanks for these things as it pleases You, God true and supreme.[51]

The death of the body was no longer to be feared or dreaded. Francis sings:

> Blessed are those whom death would find in Your most holy will, for the second death shall do them no harm.[52]

Death is a 'sister', an instrument of God's presence, a glorious moment, celebrated to this day on the feast of the Transitus of St Francis. Francis was inspired by John's words about death: Death is a self-giving act of love that loves all the way to the end (Jn 13:1); Jesus draws all people to himself (cf. Jn 12:32); It is this same suffering, sacrifice in love, with which Jesus as Father loves the world that he has created (Jn 3:16, cf. 1:1-3) and by which he enacts his cosmic purposes there (Jn 12:31). This is the glory of Jesus, the glory of the Father. Francis was willing to let go of his own plans in order to let the Creator create in him a way of peace, which has not diminished over time.

Other events in Francis' life could be equally significant; if any of the participants are of that view, they might like to share them. Similarly, it is helpful to examine the significant events in our own lives, and to evaluate their impact. Sometimes it is the events that seem to be almost bordering on failure or disappointment that open to us the most authentic reality and hope.

Points to Ponder

- It would have been easy initially for Francis and Clare to return to their families – their misdemeanours might have been forgotten, and they could have picked up where they left off.
- How would both of them have felt initially in terms of the break of relationship with family?
- Are you capable of life decisions that will be disapproved of or opposed by others because you see them as a necessary part of your journey in life in terms of God's will?
- Have you any real-life examples?
- Have you any examples from fiction that vividly outline the pain of such a dilemma?

SIGNIFICANT EVENTS IN THE LIFE OF CLARE

Reflection 15
Palm Sunday, 18 March 1212
Clare went to church to take part in the day's solemn rites with the other women. The church must have been that of San Rufino, since the Rufino bishop was the celebrant there. In her festive apparel she was beautiful and elegant, as befitted a noble girl.

That night she made her definitive decision, probably in some haste if not indeed abruptly, since her normal chaperone, Bona di Guelfuccio, was in Rome. In her place was her sister, Pacifica di Guelfuccio, according to the canonisation documents. In reality, there must have existed a small but genuine conspiracy among these women, perhaps a holy one, but one that was none-the-less concrete and effective.[53]

They had to go by the back door, and her biography indicates that amazing force had to be exerted to open the door. Clare then:

left her home, her city and her family and made haste for Saint Mary of the Portiuncula, about two kilometres from San Rufino.... [At the Portiuncula] that night it must have been crowded.[54]

... the brothers received her as they were holding a holy vigil at the Lord's altar with candles burning. She immediately cast off the filth of Babylon and addressed her farewell letter to the world. She then enacted a symbolic deed, decisive and painfully serious in those times; she shed her hair. Francis himself did the cutting as is testified in the bull of canonisation. Clare then rid herself of the fine garments and jewellery of a noble maiden in order to put on the rough habit that the friar wore.[55]

Points to Ponder
- What kind of decision did Clare make (considering her status as a noblewoman)?
- Have you ever made such a decision?
- Are you prepared to take such risks?
- Is it important to be able and willing to take risks? Why?

Reflection 16

Staying at convents of the Benedictine order and the move to San Damiano

Where was Clare to stay after she had run away from her family? The problem was solved for the moment,

> ...by sending her to stay with the Benedictine nuns of St Paul at Bastia, about four kilometres from Assisi on the road to Perugia. Her relatives reached her there, reproached her for her action, and pleaded with her through flattery and threats to return home. Clare simply uncovered her shorn hair and displayed her symbolic deed clearly in order to confirm the irrevocable firmness of her commitment. Her loved ones, although saddened and disappointed, nonetheless had to adjust themselves to the reality and did not react with the harshness that Pietro Bernardone had shown towards Francis.[56]

However, it was a different story when, one by one, Clare's family, the house of Favorone, over a short period, started to lose some of its members to religion. Whether or not because of this family turmoil, Clare soon left the convent of St Paul of Bastia in order to transfer to another, also Benedictine. It was Saint Angelo de Panzo.

Eventually, the church that Francis had built for himself, San Damiano, was prepared for Clare because, unlike the two monasteries, it was under the jurisdiction of Guido, the Bishop of Assisi, who, on many occasions, had supported Francis.

> He was a man possessed of energy and prestige, determined above all to let no one disregard his authority. The *pauperos dominae* [the poor ladies of San Damiano], as they soon came to be called, could at least consider

themselves to be safe. Now they could dedicate themselves to their life of penance, prayer and work.[57]

Points to Ponder

• Sometimes, following the gospel may bring division within families. Have you ever thought that following Christ might involve a rupture of precious family ties? How? Where? When?

Reflection 17
The conversion of Agnes

> The 'conspiracy' was still in force – and the result this time was a furious reaction on the part of her relatives. If, as it seems, her father and mother stayed in the background, her uncle, Monaldo, did not succeed in containing his rage. As soon as he learned where the two sisters were staying, he burst upon them with twelve soldiers in order to cart them back home. He found them, however, unyielding. Nor did he succeed in picking them up bodily – at least the *Vita*, the only source on this point, tells it this way – and when the uncle, foaming with rage, tried to strike Agnes, his hand was held back. Clare then intervened to plead with her relatives to halt the unjust violence and to entrust Agnes to her care.[58]

And Agnes was taken in, and she undertook the same ritual as that performed for Clare.

Points to Ponder

• What kind of decision did both Francis and Clare make that made their families so irate with them?
• What had they done, particularly in the view of the menfolk, to the status of those families?

- Reflect on public fame at the time of Francis and Clare. Have we similar constraints and obstacles in the way of making a life-giving and fruitful decision?

Reflection 18
The Saracens are miraculously put to flight
This is a part of the legend that would have been written of necessity for the process of canonisation of a saint during the Middle Ages. In this case, it concerns the invading Saracens, who are miraculously put to flight.

> The Spoleto Valley more often drank of the Chalice of Wrath [Rev 14.10] because of that scourge the Church had to endure in various parts of the world under Frederick the emperor. In it there was a battle array of soldiers and Saracen archers swarming like bees at the imperial command to depopulate its villages and to spoil its cities.[59]

> She with an undaunted heart ordered that she be brought, sick as she was, to the door and placed there before the enemy while the silver pyx enclosed in ivory in which the Body of the Holy of Holies was most devotedly reserved, preceded her.[60]

> When she had thoroughly prostrated herself to the Lord in prayer, she said to her Christ with tears (in her eyes), 'Look, my Lord, do you wish to deliver into the hand of pagans your defenceless servants whom you have nourished with your own love? Lord, I beg you, defend these, Your servants, whom I am not able to defend at this time.[61]

> Suddenly a voice from the mercy-seat of new grace, as if of a little child, resounded in her ears, 'I will always defend

you.' 'My Lord,' she said, 'please protect this city, which for Your love sustains us.' And Christ said to her, 'It will suffer afflictions, but will be defended by my protection.'[62]

The legend records that the Saracens were driven away by the power of the one who was praying, departing in haste over the walls that they had scaled.

Points to Ponder

• Clare trusted. She 'let go' of many things in order to trust God and give God the freedom to protect her. How much do we really trust in God to protect us? What kind of freedom do we give God to act as our protector in all aspects of our life?

• The Crusades may not have advanced the cause of Christ but hindered it. Is it true in history that those who lived by the sword perished by the sword? What kind of protection is given by armies?

Reflection 19

Clare's alleged influence in the city of Assisi and her freeing of that city

Clare's reputation and presence were felt far beyond San Damiano. In fact, Clare never regarded San Damiano as an enclosure in the sense that the sisters' presence or influence would be confined to it. The whole world was present in San Damiano, because she, like Francis, believed herself to be in touch with the Father of all creation, and related to all creation. So the miracle of the liberation of the city was due to a presence felt in Assisi outside the actual enclosure of San Damiano.

And another time Vitalis D'Aversa, captain of an imperial army, a man craving glory and bold in battle, directed that army against Assisi. He stripped the land of trees, devastated the entire countryside and so settled down to besiege the city. He declared with threatening words that he would, in no way, withdraw until he had taken possession of that city. It had already come to the point that danger to the city was feared imminent.

When Clare, the servant of Christ, heard this, she was profoundly grieved, called her sisters around her and said, 'Dearest children, every day we receive many good things from that city. It will be terrible if at a proper time we did not help it, as we now can.' She commanded that some ashes be brought in and that the sisters bare their heads. First she scattered a lot of ashes over her own head and then placed them on the heads of those sisters. 'Go to our Lord,' she said, 'and with all your heart beg for the liberation of the city.'

On the following morning, the merciful God brought about a happy ending to the trials, so that after the entire army had been dispersed, the proud man departed contrary to his vow and never again disturbed that land.[63]

We find that her reputation was such that people felt safe in her presence and in the presence of the poor sisters of San Damiano. And these are all events that show, in Clare's life, a God who is ultimately in control in the events of our lives and in our decisions.

The event of Frederick II's troops entering the monastery cloister can quite definitely be dated 1240:

In that year, the Emperor Frederick II, by now excommunicated for the second time, tried to impose his authority on the whole Italian peninsula. In the vale of Umbria, he was particularly anxious to gain Assisi, once a bulwark for his imperial army but now independent and pursuing a pro-papal policy.[64]

The date of the miracle of liberation from the troops of Vitalis di Aversa became an official feast for the commune of Assisi, and the cult of Clare became (perhaps even more than that of Francis), a symbol of the unity and concord of the whole city.[65]

Reflection 20
Papal approbation of the Rule

The Rule of life within Clare's community was unusual since she sought and got from Rome the privilege of poverty – 'the privilege of living without any privileges'. She changed the whole atmosphere of any constitutions that they might have received from Cardinal Ugolino, their patron. One could say it was really her Rule that eventually was approved just shortly before her death. It was this privilege, *privilegium paupertatis,* that gave the secret and the spirit to the whole Rule.

> Clare wanted to introduce into the harshness of Ugolino's constitutions concessions that are… the expression of a completely different concept of the life of apartness.

> For Ugolino, the choice of religious life is an option for seclusion, self-mortification, the denial of the very functions of life like seeing and hearing. For Clare, religious life is the exact opposite; it is the fulfilment of the life of a man or a woman. Seclusion for her is really openness to the world, isolation is the fullness of spiritual communion.

Within this paradoxical gospel perspective, the little space of San Damiano contains the whole world; the tiny cloister holds, within itself, infinite space.[66]

Points to Ponder
* Do I value the love expressed in the physical death and suffering of Christ on the cross?
* Is it healing for me?

Reflection 21
Changing direction – being drawn to the lowly
God is drawn to people of apparently little or no account just as we are drawn to people of apparent distinction. God's direction of movement is quite contrary to ours.

Martin Luther describes this contrast in one of his finest writings, in his exposition of the Magnificat (1523):

> This is our daily experience, how everyone strains only after honour, power, majesty, the good life, and everything that is just and high. And where there are just people everyone attaches himself to them, everyone runs to them, everyone serves them gladly, everyone wishes to be there, and share in their greatness. So, it is no accident that in the scriptures, few kings and princes are described as pious. Again, no one is willing to look into the depths, where there is poverty, shame, distress, suffering and anxiety; there, everyone turns away his eyes. And where such people are, everyone runs away, people flee from them and leave them. No one thinks of helping them, of standing up for them and making people consider them; so, they have to remain in the depths, and in the base, despised crowd. There is here no Creator among men who is willing to make something of nothing, although Paul says and teaches (Rom 12:16), 'Dear Brothers, Do not be haughty, but associate with the lowly.'

In our society, too, there is the wish to be important and to associate, if possible, with the mighty. Children are given this value system also. Is it any wonder then that various manifestations of neurosis arise out of the experience of inferiority and failure that many people are subjected to? If we did not move in contradiction to God's will, but in the same direction, then we would be free to take the part of those of no account.

That means simply this: We must treat others with the kindness that makes life worth living. This is the central proposition of the gospel. Being merciful and just to each other in imitation of the living God is life-giving. This is the opposite of what we have usually assimilated, i.e., that what counts is status, money, possessions, achievement, high standing in society. These latter 'achievements', on the contrary, can insulate and blind us to what really fulfils. We come to life, indeed to live, when others are merciful to us and are there to help us, not because we might repay them, but simply because they are not willing to leave us alone, because they wish us to share in their life. 'I came in order that they have life.'

Points to Ponder

- Where are gospel values such as poverty, sharing, simplicity, love, forgiveness, compassion, respect, hope, hospitality, humility lived?
- Have you experienced the living of gospel values in any way in any group of people anywhere in the world?
- Have any particular group of people in the present day come close to this?
- In what ways do we betray Jesus/betray the gospel?
- We may be unfaithful, but he is always faithful, for he cannot disown his own self (2 Tim 2:13).

SISTERHOOD AND BROTHERHOOD

By the hidden and loving mystery of God's design, men are joined together in the bonds of supernatural solidarity, so much so that the sin of one harms the others just as the holiness of one benefits the other. Penance always entails reconciliation with our brothers and sisters who are always harmed by our sins. (*Ordre Paenitential*, 5)

KEY CONCEPTS
- Value of the Human Being
- Transformation
- Letting Go

Discussion 1
Make ready to embrace and receive the gift of God. Peace, reconciliation

> …I invite the reader to the groans of prayer through Christ crucified… so that we not believe that reading is sufficient without unction, speculation without devotion, investigation without wonder, observation without joy, work without piety, knowledge without love, understanding without humility, endeavour without divine grace….[1]

> For you know the gracious act of our Lord Jesus Christ, that for your sake he became poor, although he was rich, so that by his poverty you might become rich. (2 Cor 8:9)

There are three aspects of poverty expressed in Saint Clare's First Letter to Agnes:

Oh, blessed poverty
Who bestows eternal riches on those who love and
embrace her!
Oh, holy poverty, to those who possess and desire you
God promises the kingdom of Heaven
And offers, indeed, eternal glory and blessed life!
Oh, God-centred poverty whom the Lord Jesus Christ
Who ruled and now rules Heaven and earth,
Who spoke and things were made,
Condescended to embrace before all else![2]

Discussion 2
Exploring the idea of letting go
Often we carry fears and resentments, and sometimes it is
helpful for us to express those feelings. It is important to
consider everything that we are fearful of relinquishing,
regardless of how apparently justified we are in having those
feelings.

All of us can easily identify with how we can be damaging
the body by our attachments. Over-consumption of food or
drink can ultimately damage our health and destroy our ability
to live a full and balanced life. Equally, other kinds of
attachments can impede our freedom and destroy our decision-
making ability and our growth to true humanity. This is true of
all our emotional, intellectual, psychological, sexual, physical
and religious attachments. Can we identify them with regard to
ourselves?

In times of scarcity, people seem to crave more, rather than
having the ability to spare or to share. The manna in the desert
was wasted and went bad because people were not content with
just enough for the day. This insecurity is very deep in us.
Participants might spend time alone or with others, aided by
silence at first, in order to come to an awareness of our undue

propensity for attachments, which give us a false sense of security. Reflecting on hoarding and unnecessary acquisitions, we can try to understand why it is that we need two of some items, not one, and why it is that we never seem to have enough. We need to help one another to try to come to terms with the sense of insecurity that leads us to acquire over and above our needs, and how our sense of not having enough leads not only to wastage but to others being deprived.

Discussion 3
Freedom in forgiveness
In the parable of the unmerciful servant, the forgiveness and mercy he received did not change his way of viewing the world. His self-understanding remained unaltered by the gift he received. Our self-understanding must change if we are to appreciate that we have been shown mercy. If we experience totally the forgiveness and mercy that we have truly received, then we ourselves will become more forgiving. We must constantly recall this in order to understand and appreciate the truth.

Participants could reflect on what it means to say the world is a bad debt (cf. G. K. Chesterton). We need to return to the beginning, to start again, to plumb the depths of the mystery of God by being prepared to let go at times of that which is most precious to us (cf. Gen 22: Testing of Abraham), letting God be by being still. Then we will be able to accept and experience the forgiveness and mercy of God. The sense of indebtedness experienced by Francis applies to every person, whether he or she is aware of it or not. Once experienced, it can enable us to face and be reconciled with whatever is the 'leper' in us. Otherwise we surround ourselves with devices and attachments in order to avoid what will threaten us and make us vulnerable, broken or wounded. Participants need to have a look at their own blockages.

Francis began to understand that the roadblock to his happiness was not put up by his father or anyone else, but was in fact internal… he was pampered and somewhat of a prig who avoided things and people who were ugly. In particular, Francis found lepers to be repulsive and would not go near them…. Francis heard this call not from the image of a Christ who ruled the universe but from a Christ with nails in his hands and a lance wound in his side. That Christ was quite like the leper who was disfigured, and the object of scorn and ridicule.[3]

Discussion 4
Acceptance
If we consider the instinctive horror that must have welled up in Francis upon encountering a leper in his path, then we might begin to be able to identify the leper in our society and in our own lives. It is not unlikely that our first reaction will be to see the leper in our society as being outside the mercy, forgiveness and love of God. When we come to an understanding of what it is to be cast as 'leper', then we will understand and appreciate who God is in our lives; that God is not a vengeful judge but a God who is mercy and unconditional love.

Discussion 5
The shame culture
We need to highlight the existence of the 'shame culture'. Each society manifests this and it was also present in the culture of Francis and Clare. Some decisions entail such apparent 'shame' that they engender what is tantamount to crucifixion by society. Participants could spend some time looking at society now, what its values are and whether we go along with them. Are there people whom we believe are beyond redemption and deserve to be excommunicated from the company of humankind and from God? Whom do the media identify in

this category? What kind of people are they? Have we any foundation for calling anyone evil – as the media often feel justified in doing?

It is only God who holds each of us as lovable and valuable. How often do we value people for what they possess, for their status, for conforming to what our own notion of acceptability is? Yet this is clearly at odds with the value-system we profess as Christians.

> Do not try to combine faith in Jesus Christ, our glorified Lord, with the making of distinctions between classes of people. (Jas 2:1)

> Everyone who is tempted, is attracted and seduced by his own wrong desire. Then, the desire conceives and gives birth to sin. And, when sin is fully grown, it too has a child, and the child is death. (Jas 1:13)

Reflection 1

Our own limitations

We need to embrace the limitations in our own lives. Often this confronting of limitations and accepting them causes us to experience bitterness. It is in the acceptance of limitations that some initial bitterness is experienced, but this gives way eventually to sweetness. What we face in 'lepers', or in people akin to lepers in our own time, are our own limitations. To confront these is a quantum leap; Francis took this leap and discovered joy. It was through this reversal of values that he achieved the knowledge and experience of God's love. Francis saw that what was limited had become part of what was unlimited – the Divine.

We need to talk about relationships and about our own limitations in order to build relationships based on a fruitful reality and realise that they are the opportunity for us to grow and not be stunted. Every crisis can be an opportunity. The Chinese ideogram for crisis has two characters in it, one meaning 'breakdown' and the other 'opportunity'. All crises demand decision and choice.

Points to Ponder
• We have the potential for both 'breakdown' and opportunity within ourselves – which one is actualised depends on decisions, but not on conditions.
• Can I recall making a personal free decision?
• What is required?
• Reflect on the kind of decisions that are life-giving, creative and free.

Reflection 2
Letting go, embracing 'the leper', embracing other people
Mary Craig, an English author, decided to live and work among people in the Leonard Cheshire Home in England. These people were badly disfigured from the war, and many of them bore unsightly scars. She started this work because she had given birth to two handicapped children – one had Höhler's Syndrome, gargoylism – and the other was mongoloid. As a Catholic, she was horrified by her own fear of and distaste for their conditions. However, having lived and worked for a while with the disfigured in order to come to terms with her own circumstances, she eventually saw in her two children a gift of grace and beauty. It was then that she wrote her first book, a best-seller, to which she gave the title, *Blessings*.

St Francis wanted his friars to 'rejoice when they live among people [who are considered to be] of little worth, and who are looked down upon, among the poor and the powerless, the sick and the lepers, and the beggars by the wayside.'[4] Francis desired this because he was inspired by the love of the Lord, who had made himself poor in all things.

It is precisely this kind of acceptance of 'the Other' that triggers off the personal transformation that Francis underwent, which led him to discover that what once he had perceived as bitter could now be accepted as joy. We, too, can let go of our fears and prejudices.

Just as we need to understand our culture in terms of the 'structured feeling' of our times towards groups and individuals, so we need to try to ascertain some of the 'structured feelings' of Francis' time. Because of his statement about lepers and their importance in his conversion process, it is important to understand how people of his time felt about them.

We need to change ourselves – our hearts – and, as instruments of peace, make it easier for others to do likewise. We can create climates of acceptance, welcome, hospitality, hope.

> There is nothing outside a man which by going into him can defile him; but the things that come out of a man are what defile him. (Mk 7:15)

> Learn to live and move in the spirit. (Gal 5:16)

> The spirit yields a harvest of love, joy, peace, patience, kindness, generosity, forbearance, gentleness, faith, courtesy, temperateness, purity. Since we live by the spirit, let the spirit be our rule of life. (Gal 5:22-25)

Points to Ponder
- If we observe the mistrust, lack of patience, peace, forbearance and justice in society, how far can we really admit to giving the Spirit freedom to act and guide us daily? To what extent are we conscious of the acting of the Spirit at all?

Reflection 3
Poverty, sin and leprosy
In medieval times the cultural understanding was that leprosy was particularly connected with lust. A frequently used phrase in times past was 'the leprosy of sin'. We do not use this phrase today as it is offensive to those suffering from leprosy (Hansen's disease).

> Society saw in the leper's physical corruption the mark of moral corruption. For the physician, the mere presence of the disease might well bespeak the possibility of sinful acts. A priest, out of charity, might not be as ready as the doctor to say that one of his neighbours must have sinned. Yet at the ceremony which separated the leper from the world, he would tell the poor man that God wished to punish him for the evil he had done in this world. Likewise, in a sermon, he would explain that Jesus coming down from the mountain to heal the leper was the saviour coming from heaven to redeem sinful man. There were few in the parish who did not attach the immorality of the leper in the Bible to the lepers outside the town gate. Why shouldn't they, after all? The king had warned that for their own solace the lepers were spreading the disease among the healthy, and everyone knew that the lepers were driven by a depraved and irresistible sexual urge. The disease was emblematic of a vice-ridden soul.[5]

Medieval commentators on Scripture:

> ...link leprosy with sexual depravity. Lust was one of the deadly sins, and what is more, leprosy was commonly assumed to be a venereal disease. In accordance with that notion, Adamus Scotus (fl. 1180) writes that Naaman the

leper falls to pride and from pride into lust, 'for what is the impurity of leprosy, unless it is the sin of lust?' Tertullian (c. 160-after 200) interprets leprosy as a metaphor for adultery in his argument that the apostles did not promise a second penitence to the unchaste. Just as the biblical law (in Leviticus 13:14) states that when old leprous flesh appears, the patient must be pronounced defiled, 'So also is adultery an irremovable blemish when it returns once more from the past and sullies the purity of that new colouring from which it was effaced.' Prudentius (348-after 405), in his Peristephanon, attaches leprosy to carnal sin in his description of one who is morally deformed by spiritual leprosy.... 'This other is dragged by foul lust among public harlots and polluted with mire and filth as he goes a-begging after dirty whorings.'[6]

The leprous sinners described by Prudentius are not all sexually depraved. What is common to all, however, is their profane worldliness and the leprosy that symbolises it. Appropriately, the avaricious man had hands that permanently grasp.... 'And here is another who in his greed crooks his hands and draws them close, his palm doubled, his fingernails like hooks, and cannot relax the tendons.'[7]

The leprous symptoms of Prudentius' sinners – the sexuality, oedema, jaundice, maiming, blindness, claw hands, itching, fevers, swelling, and ulcerations – externalise the spiritual effects of their sinfulness. The passage that ends in the description of them emphasises the hideousness of their depravity:

peccante nil est taetrius,
nil tam leprosum aut putridum;
cruda est cicatrix criminum
oletque ut antrum Tartari.

(There is nothing fouler than a sinner,
nothing so leprous or rotten;
the wound of his sins keeps bleeding
and stinks like the pit of hell.)

Thus, for Prudentius, leprosy is finally not merely tied to sexual excess, or avariciousness, or anger. It is the symbol of sinfulness, or general ethical decay.[8]

Leprosy is commonly used as a figure for generalised sin.

Points to Ponder
- In society today, what is regarded as the greatest sin?
- Which are the sins that society, and the mass media, say are evil, and which call for the elimination of a person from society?
- Do these sins differ from culture to culture, from age to age?
- Would you embrace such outcasts as your brothers/sisters as your way to the acquisition of the pearl of great value?

Reflection 4
Lepers and leprosy
The stigma of leprosy is the product of a long tradition, and that tradition has survived because it is the expression of a complex array of cultural and social forces and of the seeming necessity to have scapegoats in society. On the one hand, we have the lepers themselves on the defensive because of anger at the inherent injustice to them; on the other hand, there are those in

society who want to load onto the leper all the negative qualities that can show in human nature. Therefore, not only the disease, but every other shortcoming is heaped onto the leper. It is thus regarded as a disease of character and of soul.

Points to Ponder

- Do we have outcasts and/or scapegoats in today's society?
- Is it possible that we might not recognise them?
- Do we marginalise them to such an extent that they can no longer play an active or fruitful role in society?
- Have we a compassionate system – a compassionate society?
- Is there such a thing as a caring society?

Reflection 5

The leper and society

> The leper would suffer his disease for years, and so for years be at society's mercy…. If the leper's disease was feared for its contagiousness, and if edict upon edict was passed to prevent him from mingling with society, it is nonetheless true that he was often to be seen in the marketplace and on the road…. The leper was by turns the object of vilification and of sympathy. A physician could assure the leper himself that his disease was a sign that God had chosen to grant his soul salvation, but he might simultaneously include in his diagnosis that his patient was morally corrupt.[9]

> The Church might similarly decree that leprosy was a gift of God, but its bishops and priests would nonetheless use the disease as a metaphor for spiritual degeneration. The leper was seen as sinful and meritorious, as punished by God and as given special grace by Him.[10]

Normally, the separation from society of the person diagnosed as a leper began 'with public accusation by neighbours'. The Church, in the person of the priest, had to initiate the necessary action in accordance with what is laid down in the Book of Leviticus.

Separation

> In 1179, the third Lateran council issued a decree which urged that the segregation of lepers from society be accompanied by appropriate ceremony. The decree provided a number of specimen rituals, and the *separatio leprosorum* in time came to be accepted widely, though not universally, for lepers continued to be treated with varying rigour.[11]

> In all the territory of ancient Gaul – the rituals of separation were similar. In removing the leper from the world, the ceremonies differed little from the office for the dead, for in principle the leper was no longer one of the living.[12]

Points to Ponder
• The Church can at times bless and ritualise dubious events, for example, aircraft preparing for the bombing of Hiroshima, Nagasaki, etc. My faith and belief is in God – sometimes that faith has to challenge existing practices in Church and State. Francis and Clare challenged society and the Church by their lives. Can we see ourselves as being that free and that courageous?

Reflection 6

The solemn ceremony of separation

[1] During the ceremony the leper knelt before the altar beneath a black cloth supported by two trestles. (However, at Amiens and elsewhere, he was required to stand in a grave in a cemetery.)

[2] His face was covered by a black veil as he heard the Mass.

[3] The officiating priest threw a spadeful of earth from the cemetery on the head of the leper three times, explaining that the ritual symbolises the death of the leper to the world.

[4] The priest said, 'Be dead to the world, be reborn to God', and the leper replied, 'O Jesus, my redeemer, you formed me out of earth, you dressed me in a body; let me be reborn in the final day.'

[5] Then, using the vernacular, the priest read the prohibitions that made the alienation of the victim explicit:

I forbid you to ever enter the church or monastery, fair, mill, marketplace, or company of persons. I forbid you to ever leave your house without your leper's costume, in order that one recognise you, and that you never go barefoot. I forbid you to wash your hands or anything about you in the stream or in the fountain and to ever drink; and if you wish water to drink, fetch it in your cask or porringer. I forbid you to touch anything you bargain for or buy until it is yours. I forbid you to enter a tavern. If you want wine, whether you buy it or someone gives it to you, have it put in your cask. I forbid you to live with any woman other than your own. I forbid you, if you go on the road and you meet some person who speaks to you, to fail to put yourself downwind before you answer. I forbid you to go in a narrow lane, so that should you meet any person, he should not be able to catch the affliction from you. I forbid you, if you go along any thoroughfare, to ever touch a well or the cord unless you have put on your gloves. I forbid you to ever touch children or to give them anything. I forbid you to eat or drink from any dishes other than your own. I forbid you drinking or eating in company, unless with lepers.

[6]   Following the reading of the proscriptions, the leper put on his costume and was given the signal with which he was to warn the healthy of his approach. Both signal and costume varied with locality. The instrument for warning the populace of the leper's approach was usually a rattle or castanet, but it was sometimes a bell, either carried or worn on the shoes.[13]

[7]   The priest would bless the outcast's utensils and encourage him to be patient. The ritual of St Albin d'Angers directs the cleric to say: 'Because of greatly having to suffer sadness, tribulation, disease, leprosy, and other worldly adversity, one reaches the kingdom of paradise, where there is neither disease nor adversity, but all are pure and spotless, without filth and without any stain of filth, more resplendent than the sun, where you will go, if it please God. But so that you be a good Christian and so that you bear this adversity patiently, God gives you grace.'[14]

[8]   The priest would next place a cross before the leper's door, hang a box for alms on the cross, and place an offering in

it, … to provide liberally for his needs. The congregation would presumably follow the priest's example and place alms in the leper's cup.[15]

This was the procedure used normally in a large portion of Europe. Deviations from the procedure of course occurred. The lepers were sometimes dealt with brutally, even murdered.

Several highly placed lepraphobes, including Henry II of England, his great-grandson Edward I, and Philip V of France, took the position that the recommended ritual was unnecessarily symbolical. The revisions instituted by Henry and Philip were similar. Both chose to replace the religious service with a simple civil ceremony. It consisted of strapping the leper to a post and setting him afire. Edward adhered a trifle more closely to the letter of the ecumenical degree. Lepers, during his reign, were permitted the comforts of a Christian funeral. They were led down to the cemetery and were burned alive.[16]

…since the medieval leper could not count on a miraculous cure, the diagnosis of his disease was usually a prediction of lifelong suffering and isolation.[17]

The asylums which confined the leper were intended to assure his separation. Nearly always, they were located outside cities and towns, away from centres of human activity, and should the town expand around it, the leprosarium would be moved…. Whenever possible, the asylums were built downwind from the town, so that the prevailing wind did not pass first over the leprosarium and then over the town.[18]

In its simplest form, the asylum a village would build for
one leper would be a small wooden cottage, elevated on
four props and surrounded by a fence. When the diseased
were numerous, their huts and the cultivated land around
the buildings would be located in an enclosure. The Third
Lateran Council provided that asylums of this size should
have their own chapel, cemetery, and priest. In time, stone
buildings might be constructed, either on the same plan as
the wooden huts or else much larger and divided into small
cubicles for individual lepers. Within a single leprosarium,
the rich could live in private dwellings while the poor were
crowded together....

...most of the asylum's land was given over to farming, and
so a cowshed, a sheepfold, a barn, an enclosure for pigs,
and other farm buildings were on the property. The
community, which had two groups of brethren (the lepers
and the members of religious orders) lived in two separate
buildings. The lepers' building had a kitchen and a
refectory, the refectory, which also served as sleeping
quarters, had a fireplace and eight beds.[19]

...the asylums were established to confine lepers (and so
the disease) and to keep them alive; Leper houses were
hospitals in the sense that they were institutions for the
reception of the sick, and in some leper houses there were
nurses to dress the sores of the lepers; but on the whole,
leper houses were rather combinations of the prison, the
monastery, and the almshouse than hospitals in the
modern sense. The primary function of the leper house
was to form a prison, or, if we prefer the term, a
compulsory isolation hospital, for the seclusion of the
lepers from the general population.[20]

A lot of leprosaria were run by religious, but bit by bit city magistrates took them over. In religious-run leprosaria, for instance the asylum at Illeford, the lepers also took the monastic vows of poverty, chastity and obedience! (This contrasts with the attitude of Francis towards them.) In 1346, the Bishop of London directed that they say the divine office – something very difficult for anybody, but particularly for lepers already having the burden of being excluded from society and separated within the asylum. There were difficulties with regard to marriage in the case of the leper as well. So mortification of the spirit and of the body was a consequence of such rule. The leper was a threat to society and a carrier of contagion, and thus was put in the position of a beggar, genuinely reliant on the goodwill of other people. It was common too, and typical, that the leper was denied all or part of the privileges of ownership, so that he couldn't really take his estate with him or be left an estate. The laws tended to uphold the principle that leprosy denies a leper the usual rights of ownership.

> Thus, in any locality where the leper lost the privileges both of retaining and distributing his estate, a person might be put in a leper house so that the seigneur could gain profit or vengeance.[21]

> ...the law could place a person outside of society by depriving him of his rights to marry or to stay married, and to own and transmit property. It could simply and effectively deprive the leper of the right to have a home, and that being so, it could compel him to depend upon the very society which, out of loathing and fear, wrote those laws. Under such circumstances, the best the leper could do would be to turn from the world and enter the closed

society of the leprosarium. There, at last, he would have a bed and food. The prison could also be a refuge.[22]

Points to Ponder
• For Francis, embracing the leper and then 'becoming' the leper was the definitive step in his following of Christ. Why?

Reflection 7
Detachment – asceticism

I say that detachment sometimes sounds like an empty, uncreative, and deadening state. If I seek evidence for this, however, I find that nothing could be further from the truth. I can look at the life of Jesus or at the lives of the most truly free people I know, or I can simply reflect upon the taste of real spiritual freedom I have experienced in my own life. Always the evidence is the same; true freedom from attachment is characterised by great, unbounded love, endless creative energy, and deep, pervasive joy. Nor need I worry about freedom from addiction taking suffering or caring out of life, for compassion takes the place of attachment. Where there was the agony of clinging to and grasping one's attachments, freedom brings a feeling of unity with the pain of the world. I think we have all had tastes of this. It is a clean, bright pain. In a way it is more deep and sharp than any addiction agony, because it is so real. But there is no despair in it. It is filled with hope.[23]

Points to Ponder
• What does the above passage mean to you?

Reflection 8

Being sorry, self-discipline, undergoing hardships, turning away from materialism

Many people feel a real need for more self-discipline in their lives and are puzzled as to how they should set about it. We know well that it can be almost impossible to break habits of over-indulgence without a certain pendulum swing, and we should not despise this method. The extremes of our folly can become the boundaries of our hunger for God, so it is good and helpful to fast, to be uncomplainingly cold or hot or uncomfortable, to cut back on sleep, and, above all, not to talk about these things. Sooner or later, common sense asserts itself and we become more aware of the bad temper which follows fasting and sleeplessness, and the subtle pride which accompanies them. The story was told by Hubert Van Zeller, OSB, of a certain man who once said to himself: 'I am probably the only man in Reading Station in a hair shirt,' and realised that he should take if off as soon as possible! Such moments of truth will come to us all. Like the 'certain man', we must avoid falling into one weakness (smugness) while we are escaping another (the unspecified reason for the hair shirt).

We may also come to realise that our thrust towards penance is partly rooted in self-hatred or hatred of our humanity. Most of us have negative hang-ups of one sort or another, and as we move more seriously into our life of prayer, they will tend to be thrown to the surface. It will help if we realise that this is a good sign, not a cause for anxiety, because it indicates that our prayer is seeping down to the layers which need healing and redemption. So we are not more neurotic because we have begun to pray, but we may appear to be, because when we start praying regularly, our negative attitudes, which were previously cemented over, begin to push to the surface. To some extent, this never ends; it is almost as if we are constantly in the process of being created, so that there is always more of us to be brought to God. Even in the last two years of his life, after he had received the stigmata, Celano tells us that Francis still did not consider that he had laid hold of his goal, but was still hoping to make a start [1 Cel, 103]. Even on his deathbed, he was saying: 'Let us now begin to serve God, because up to now we have done nothing.'[24]

Points to Ponder
- In the course of a lifetime we never really arrive at our goal – what are the implications of this for us?
- How does it make you feel at this time?

Reflection 9
Trust must be real and open to experience
Abstractions that sound sophisticated can in hindsight become jargon, with little understanding or relation to reality. Consider the following statement by Frank O'Connor:

> I wasn't really writing about any woman in particular…but about that side of women that appealed to me – the one that has no patience with abstractions. I, of course, was full of abstractions.[25]

We have so often substituted knowledge of formulas or rules for real faith. Tradition always emphasises the faith by which one believes and the continuous growth of that faith. Both became one in the maturing of Francis and Clare, and this is a normal maturing of faith, which is meant to apply to all of us.

Points to Ponder
- How did Francis and Clare integrate the two aspects of faith – belief and continuous growth?
- What does *separation* or imbalance do in our own maturing of faith?
- What are the consequences of accepting only one aspect as the total reality of faith?

Reflection 10
Asceticism – penance, fasting

Another extremely important aspect of penance, fasting and generally cutting back, is the implicit solidarity with those who have less than we do. Francis said once: 'It makes me very ashamed when I find a man who is poorer than myself.'[26]

Admittedly he had taken a vow to have nothing of his own, but he speaks for us all in some measure. Through fasting we commit ourselves to co-operate with Christ as he works to make the world the way it was meant to be, because we assist in this process, even by the smallest and simplest restoration of a balance due in justice. There is still enough food for everyone if we would only cut back and share; our fasting is nothing compared with the permanent malnourishment of more than half the world. Both Francis and Clare, who saw that everything on the earth is God's gift, given equally to each of us, considered that they were stealing if they had more than they needed while others did not have enough. This is what Francis meant by saying that he felt indicted when he met someone who had less than he. The message of this attitude in the light of today's injustices needs no spelling out.[27]

Some of our sisters and brothers are starving now, while we have too much to eat and too many choices. While some of our brothers and sisters have the problem of deciding, 'Which restaurant will we choose this evening?', others are wondering, 'When next will we see or taste a morsel of food?'

Jesus was free to relate intimately to all, in particular the most needy. He chose to serve the greatest need and, therefore, he chose to be detached so as to be free to serve.

Francis frequently uses the term 'mother'. He was seen by Clare in a vision as mother. His understanding of the female attributes and their necessity for good relationships is apparent from Chapter six of his later Rule: 'Let each one confidently make known his need to the other, for if a mother loves and cares for her son according to the flesh, how much more diligently must someone love and care for his Brother according to the Spirit.'[28]

Points to Ponder
* Francis frequently uses the term 'mother'. He was seen by Clare in a vision as mother.
* How do you feel about Jesus being 'mother'?

Reflection 11
My vocation to become father, mother, sister, brother

As long as the Father evokes fear, he remains an outsider and cannot dwell within me. But Rembrandt, who showed me the father in utmost vulnerability, made me come to the awareness that my final vocation is indeed to become like the father, and to live out his divine compassion in my daily life. Though I am both the younger son and the eldest son, I am not to remain them, but to become the father. No father or mother ever became father or mother without having been son or daughter, but every son and daughter has to consciously choose to step beyond their childhood and become father and mother for others. It is a hard and lonely step to take, especially in a period of history in which parenthood is so hard to live well – but it is a step that is essential for the fulfilment of the spiritual journey.[29]

Points to Ponder

- In the writings of Francis and Clare, the term 'mother' is often used when referring to females, and the term 'brother' when referring to males.
- Males: How does it feel to be called to be mother? What does it evoke in you?
- Females: How does it feel to be called to be brother: what does it evoke in you?

Reflection 12
Grief, forgiveness, generosity

Grief

I am beginning to see that much of praying is grieving. This grief is so deep not just because the human sin is so great, but also... and more so... because the divine love is so boundless. To become like the father whose only authority is compassion, I have to shed countless tears and so prepare my heart to receive anyone, whatever their journey has been, and forgive them from that heart.[30]

Forgiving

The second way that leads to spiritual fatherhood is forgiveness. It is through constant forgiveness that we become like the Father. Forgiveness from the heart is very, very difficult. It is next to impossible. Jesus said to his disciples: 'When your brother wrongs you seven times a day and seven times comes back to you and says 'I am sorry,' you must forgive him.' (Cf. Mt 18:21, 22)

I have often said 'I forgive you', but even as I said these words my heart remained angry or resentful. I still wanted to hear the story that tells that I was right after all; I still wanted to hear apologies and excuses; I still wanted the satisfaction of receiving some praise in return – if only the praise for being so forgiving![31]

Generosity

The third way to become like the father is generosity. In the parable, the father not only gives his departing son everything he asks, but also showers him with gifts on his return. And to his elder son, he says 'All I have is yours.' There is nothing the father keeps for himself. He pours himself out for his sons. In order to become like the father, I must be as generous as the father is generous. Just as the father gives his very self to his children, so must I give my very self to my brothers and sisters. Jesus makes it very clear that it is precisely this giving of self that is the mark of the true disciple. No one can have greater love than to lay down his life for his friends. This giving of self is a discipline because it is something that does not come spontaneously. As children of the darkness that rules through fear, self-interest, greed, and power, our great motivators are survival and self-preservation.

But as children of the light who know that perfect love casts out all fear it becomes possible to give away all that we have for others.[32]

Every time I take a step in the direction of generosity, I know that I am moving from fear to love. This transformation leads me to the fulfilment of the deepest desire of my restless heart. Because what greater joy can there be for me than to stretch out my tired arms, and let my hands rest in a blessing on the shoulders of my homecoming children?[33]

Points to Ponder

* Would I wish to be given the gift of tears?
* How can I try to be a forgiving person, or at least not resort to blaming and accusing others?
* How generous am I prepared to be – is my generosity conditioned?
* Do I limit my giving so as to control what I will share with others?

Reflection 13
The poverty of God's non-demanding love

True fatherhood is sharing the poverty of God's non-demanding love. I am afraid to enter into that poverty, but those who have already entered it through their physical or mental disabilities will be my teachers. Looking at the people I live with, the handicapped men and women as well as their assistants, I see the immense desire for a father in whom fatherhood and motherhood are one. They all have suffered from the experience of rejection or abandonment; they all have been wounded as they grew up; they all wonder whether they are worthy of the unconditional love of God, and they all search for the place where they can safely return and be touched by hands that bless them. Rembrandt portrays the father as the man who has transcended the ways of his children. His own loneliness and anger may have been there, but they have been transformed by suffering and tears. His loneliness has become endless solitude, his anger boundless gratitude. This is who I have to become. I see as clearly as I can see the immense beauty of the father's emptiness and compassion. Can I let the younger and the elder son grow in me to the maturity of the compassionate father? When, four years ago, I went to St Petersburg to see Rembrandt's *The Return of the Prodigal Son,* I had little idea how much I would have to live what I then saw. I stand with awe at the place where Rembrandt brought me. He led me from the kneeling, dishevelled young son to the standing, bent-over father, from the place of being blessed to the place of blessing. As I look at my own ageing hands, I know that they have been given to me to stretch out towards all who suffer, to rest upon the shoulders of all who come, and to offer the blessing that emerges from the immensity of God's love.[34]

Points to Ponder
• How might we allow God to show himself to us as God of mercy and love?
• Why might we prefer another kind of God?

Reflection 14
Relationships: mother, father, sister, brother, daughter, son
The Man Jesus – its ultimate significance

> His ability to speak as liberator does not reside in his maleness, but in the fact that he has renounced this system of domination and seeks to embody in his person the new humanity of *service* and *mutual empowerment*.[35]

St Clare, in her to letter to Agnes,[36] tells her that she should in fact look at the vision of God as it is expressed in the humanity of Christ, as a mirror without blemish, and that in that mirror she will see what poverty is. As she looks in the mirror she will behold the poverty of him who was placed in a manger, the marvellous humility, the astonishing poverty, the King of Angels.[37]

23. Then in the depths of this same mirror, contemplate the ineffable charity which led Him to suffer on the wood of the cross, and die thereon the most shameful kind of death.

24. Therefore, that Mirror, suspended on the wood of the cross, urged those who passed by to consider, saying

25. 'All you who pass by the way, look and see if there is any suffering like My suffering' [Lam 1:12]

26. Let us answer Him with one voice and spirit as He said, 'Remembering this over and over leaves my soul downcast within me!' [Lam 3:20]

27. From this moment then, O Queen of our Heavenly

King, let yourself be inflamed more strongly with the fervour of charity.

28. [As you] contemplate further His ineffable delights, eternal riches and honours,

29. and sigh for them in the great desire and love of your heart, may you cry out:

30. 'Draw me after you. We will run in the fragrance of your perfumes, O heavenly Spouse.'[38]

Clare is reminding Agnes that, seeing Christ on the cross, she should see herself as beloved by him to the extent that she is joined with him on the cross. Ruth Page, in her book *The Incarnation of Freedom and Love,* writes:

> The first thing which may be sympathetic to the idea of a female Christ, to what Reuther calls 'Christ in the form of our sister' was a poem written by a woman who had been brutally raped, and who therefore was insecure in relation toward men. In her case, male sexuality was precisely the origin of un-freedom and un-love, so there was no hope in looking to a male Christ for salvation. It was on seeing the representation of a female figure on the Cross that the woman began to be healed.[39]

We can conclude this reflection with a poem that records her experience of salvation, which the presentation of Christ as woman mirrored to her. Ruth Page came across this anonymous poem in a newsletter:

O God
Through the image of a woman
Crucified on the Cross
I understand at last.

For over half of my life
I have been ashamed
Of the scars I bear.
These scars tell an ugly story,
A common story,
About a girl who was the victim
When a man acts out his fantasies.

In the warmth, peace and sunlight of your presence
I was able to uncover the tightly clenched fists
For the first time.
I felt your suffering presence within me
In that event.
I have known you as a vulnerable baby,
As a brother,
And as a father.
Now I know you as a woman.

You were there with me

As the violated girl
Caught in helpless suffering.

The chains of shame and fear
No longer bind my heart and body.
A slow fire of compassion and forgiveness
Is enkindled.
My tears fall now
For men as well as women.

You, God
Can make our violated bodies
Vessels of love and comfort
To such a desperate man.
I am honoured
To carry this womanly power
Within my body and soul.

You are not ashamed of your wounds.
You showed them to Thomas
As marks of your ordeal and death.
I will no longer hide these wounds of mine.
I will bear them gracefully.
They tell a resurrection story.

Points to Ponder

- Can I accept a God incarnate, who suffers, who is vulnerable, who weeps with those who mourn?
- Do I respect a God who loves, who decides to become weak?
- Why might I resist such a God?
- Recall an occasion when you have faced a complicated decision – when what was right or wrong was not easy for you to decide.
- 'As she looks in the mirror...' In your opinion, what is Clare trying to get across to Agnes?
- What presentation of Christ is she giving to Agnes?

Reflection 15
Desert experience

Any struggle with addiction is a desert because it involves deprivation. If our motivations are primarily utilitarian, this deprivation may consist only of the denial of one specific object of attachment; trying to do without so much food, trying to give up tobacco, and so on. With major addictions or more conscious spiritual motivations, the desert can grow to encompass all of life: every habit may be exposed to the searing, purifying sun; every false prop is vulnerable to relinquishment; and one can be left truly dependent upon the grace of God for sustenance. Most of our deserts lie somewhere between these extremes, and most of the time we do little more than dance around their edges. All the same, deserts enrich our lives immeasurably. Each desert holds seeds of repentance, possibilities of recognising how mixed our motives really are. And, with the reign of grace, each desert holds the possibility of our reclaiming our true heart's desire. Even if we only touch their edges, our deserts teach us about the limits of our personal power, and point us toward that constant centre of ourselves where our dignity is found in our dependence upon God.[40]

Points to Ponder

- Promise yourself an experience of desert-like solitude, if not now, then at some point in the future.

Reflection 16
From Mother Theresa of Calcutta:

> I have accepted the responsibility of representing the poor of the world, the unwanted, the unloved, the uncared for, the crippled, the blind, the lepers, the alcoholics, the people thrown away by society, the people who have forgotten what human love is or what the human touch is.

I have come to realise more and more that the greatest disease and the greatest suffering is to be unwanted, unloved, uncared for, to be shunned by everybody, to be just nobody…. Compassion and love have to grow from within, from our union with Christ.[41]

Points to Ponder
- How do I cope with my loneliness if I have reflected on the pathways chosen by Francis and Clare?
- What difference does a Mother Theresa of Calcutta and her approach to human beings as cited above make in realistic terms to the world today?
- If people in the many troubled areas in the world today were transformed into having her attitude, would it make a difference? How?

Reflection 17
Are we really interested in others' needs?
When asked to explain the tearing down of housing vacated by the US Army in the Presidio in San Francisco, a State representative said, in explanation:

The reason for tearing the housing down is to enhance the recreation park of the Presidio. The park does belong to all the people of the United States. They have a right to have a nice experience when they go there![42]

There are 76,000 homeless people in the area where the park is situated, yet this is the wealthiest location in the United States.

Points to Ponder
- Who are the 'people' that the representative is referring to?

- Who are those who have a right to expect a 'nice experience' when they go there? Do all people receive equal recognition, or do some people not exist?
- What are the 'bricks' that build a lasting peace?
- How can I help? In the light of the gospel, what am I called to do?

EUCHARIST

God's Compassionate Presence

Each participant has been called to this time and place; and all participants are also called together as a group. In the context of a celebration of the Eucharist, they should see themselves as called to be sisters and brothers in Christ. This realisation will help them to trust, to be poor with one another, to share, to be upbuilding of one another: in effect, 'to wash one another's feet'. Arising out of their sharing, they will come to know themselves as belonging in the love of God in the same way as Francis and Clare, and their brothers and sisters, belong.

Francis uses the idea of a mother's love, which, like the embracing of the leper, does not make distinctions. Participants can readily reflect on a mother's love, which is the analogy that Scripture uses for God's love for us. 'Can a mother forget her infant? Be without tenderness for the child of her womb? Even should she forget, I will never forget you' (Is 49:15).

A mother's love communicates to us the compassion of God and, equally, the compassion that Francis sought in the fraternity. It is worthwhile contemplating the qualities, feelings and experiences associated with that type of compassion. That can be done by reflecting and sharing as a group. The qualities of compassion, brokenness, identification, empathy and concern will be the offering in the Eucharist so that the Body and Blood of Christ can become truly ours, to the extent that we, too, make offerings of ourselves to and for one another.

The group must see the significance of becoming the Christ who is broken, who shares, who gives life. It is at this point that a meaningful celebration of the Eucharist might take place. It is recommended that the participants prepare the Eucharistic celebration themselves, if possible.

The Eucharist is an event of recall, of both present realities and future promises. The celebration of the Eucharist was always an important event in the lives of Francis and Clare.

> Remember how the Lord your God led you for forty years in the wilderness to humble you, and to test you and to know your heart. (Deut 8:2-3)

The Lord in the desert fed them. The Eucharist is a God-given meal to be shared – it is a communion.

> Because there is one bread, we who are many are one body, for we all partake of the one bread. (1 Cor 10:17)

The reality of this celebration demands the reality of sharing, not hoarding. We have to be prepared to share, to let go.

> When you meet together it is not the Lord's supper that you eat. For in eating each one goes ahead with his or her own meal and one is hungry and another drunk. (1 Cor 11:20-21)

> For if a person with gold rings on his fingers and in fine clothes comes into your assembly and a poor person in shabby clothes also comes in, and you pay attention to the one wearing the fine clothes and say 'sit here, please', while

you say to the poor one, 'stand there or sit at my feet', have you not made distinctions over yourselves and become judges with evil designs? (Js 2:2-24)

Therefore the Eucharist is a sign that expresses fellowship, sharing with one another and with Christ. It is Christ who breaks the bread and shares it, and we do likewise. Rank or status meant nothing to Jesus (cf. Mk 12: 13-14). In fact, if he acknowledged a hierarchy, an order of things, first place was given to the hungry, the needy, those who were last, those who needed their feet to be washed. How well Francis and Clare understood this. We can often listen to the voice of respectability and fail to pay attention to those who are normally ignored. We are one with humanity, we must 'Take and Eat' this bread with the poor and wretched of this world. If I eat at the table of the Lord with others, and have hatred in my heart for them, I am missing a sacrament that is intended to heal our animosities and divisions.

I hate, I despise your feasts and I take no delight in your solemn assembly.... Take away from me the noise of your songs; to the melody of your harps I will not listen. But let justice roll down like waters and righteousness like an overflowing stream. (As 5:21-24)

Our confidence in recognising the needs of others to be special, to feel respected, to be affirmed, to be needed, stems from this Eucharistic reality of 'Take and Eat', saying in effect, I give you the bread of myself. Through this we may come to a realisation of our own creaturehood and a recognition of our own strengths and weaknesses, which make up the person that I am before the Creator. Who am I in relationship? Who am I with and for others?

I carry that Bread of Life to others. I am the instrument because of the desire and love of the Creator. All of creation touches this celebration. All of creation can be affected by it.

> He made you feel hungry, he fed you with manna, that neither you or your father had known. (Deut 8:3)

How Should We Prepare this Eucharist?

Here we meditate on the Eucharistic Prayers and the movements in the Eucharist. The words of the Eucharistic Prayers most commonly used can guide us.

1. Sense of Self: Humility

Who am I?

Father – Creatures – Life – Creation, a Gift

> Father, you are holy indeed,
> and all creation rightly gives you praise.
> All life, all holiness comes from you…. (III)
> Father in heaven,
> it is right that we should give you thanks and glory:
> you alone are God, living and true…
> Source of life and goodness, you have created all things,
> to fill your creatures with every blessing
> and lead all men to the joyful vision of your light…
> You formed man in your own likeness
> and set him over the whole world
> to serve you, his creator,
> and to rule over all creatures. (IV)

We are asked to Take and Eat, Take and Drink. We receive the gift and it is meant to follow that we invite others to Take and Eat, Take and Drink.

In the Eucharist we are given an opportunity to enter into

the life of Jesus and to share in his vocation and mission. As Paul says in his speech to the Athenians at the Areopagus, 'In him we live and move and have our being' (Acts 17:28).

Greed blinds us to the needs of others as well as to our own real needs. We make ourselves the centre of the universe and of our own imagination and perceived wants.

In the Eucharist we take the bread, wine and fruit. It is blessed, broken and given to the hungry. We must not speak or hear these words unthinkingly. Let us ask for eyes that can see, ears that can hear, to experience reality with a new focus.

> The pupil of the eye is but a tiny porthole in a sea of radiation. In a universe alight with images, we are mostly in the dark.... I know that these signals are there, in the room with me, because if I flip on the radio or television, I will suddenly be able to see or hear them – in the same ways that visions suddenly 'appear' before me the minute I open my eyes. If I had still other kinds of detectors... I could pick up still other kinds of signals. Yet we walk through this dense web of radiant information every day without being in the least aware of its existence.[43]

Nuclear
It is not that he can't speak;
Who created languages
But God? Nor that he won't,
To say that is to imply
Malice. It is just that
He doesn't, or does so at times
When we are not listening, in
Ways we have yet to recognise.
As speech, we call him the dumb
God with an effrontery beyond
Pardon, whose silence so eloquent

As his? What word so explosive
As that one Palestinian
Word with the endlessness of its fallout.
(R. S. Thomas)[44]

2. Self in Relationship
'No man is an island unto himself' – John Donne
We are connected, we are not in isolation – our existence affects
others... Christ – friends – family – brothers/sisters –
acquaintances. We are affected by others. Thus, all are called
continually to self-transcendence.

Sisterhood/Brotherhood

> Father, accept this offering from your whole family...
> count us among those you have chosen. (I)
> From age to age you gather a people to yourself...
> Father, hear the prayers of the family you have gathered
> here before you.... (III)
> Remember those who take part in this offering, those here
> present and all your people, and all who seek you with a
> sincere heart....
> Father, in your mercy grant also to us, your children, to
> enter into your heavenly inheritance.... (IV)
> We, your people and your ministers, recall his passion,
> his resurrection from the dead and his ascension into glory. (I)
> Father, we acknowledge your greatness: all your actions
> show your wisdom and love... but helped all men to seek
> and find you... you sent your only Son.... that we might
> live no longer for ourselves but for him.... to complete his
> work on earth... gather all who share this one bread and
> one cup into the one Body of Christ, a living sacrifice of
> praise. (IV)

Through the Resurrection and Ascension of Jesus we come into your company as friends and as equals.

3. Self and Others in the Harmony of Peace
Needs – Responsibilities – to have and give life to others
Peace, reconciliation dialogue – self-denial
Relationships – founded on core relationship – Father, Son, Spirit
Freedom from fear, anxiety, loneliness, rejection, rootlessness: being instruments of love, belonging, esteem, self-respect, recognition, appreciation, self-actualisation... **Word Made Flesh**...
Instruments of Peace, Forgiveness, Compassion, Listening, Quality of Heart

> Father, accept this offering from your whole family.... (I)
> May all of us who share in the body and blood of Christ be brought together in unity by the Holy Spirit.... Remember our brothers and sisters who have gone to their rest in the hope of rising again.... (II) Father, hear the prayers of the family you have gathered here before you. In mercy and love unite all your children wherever they may be. (III)
> He always loved those who were his own in the world.... We offer you his body and blood, the acceptable sacrifice which brings salvation to the whole world. (IV)

> Grant us your peace in this life, save us from final damnation, and count us among those you have chosen. (I)

> We offer you in thanksgiving this holy and living sacrifice. Look with favour on your Church's offering, and

see the Victim whose death has reconciled us to yourself…. May this sacrifice, which has made our peace with you, advance the peace and salvation of all the world. (III)

Even when he disobeyed you and lost your friendship you did not abandon him to the power of death, but helped all men to seek and find you. (IV)

As Christians, we believe that Jesus, who is the truth about both God and man, gives foretastes of his Incarnation in all those fragmentary truths. We believe as well that Christ is present in any seeker after truth. Simone Weil has said that though a person may run as fast as he can away from Christ, if it is toward what he considers true, he runs in fact into the arms of Christ.[45]

The Holy Spirit unites us into one family and gathers us in friendship forever with God – three as one in love.

Asceticism of Unity = Dialogue

Prayer
Some days, although we cannot pray, a prayer
utters itself. So a woman will lift
her head from the sieve of her hands and stare
at the minims sung by a tree, a sudden gift.

Some nights, although we are faithless, the truth
enters our hearts, that small familiar pain;
then a man will stand stock-still, hearing his youth
in the distant Latin chanting of a train.
Pray for us now. Grade 1 piano scales

console the lodger looking out across
a Midlands town. Then dusk, and someone calls
a child's name as though they named their loss.
Darkness outside. Inside, the radio's prayer –
Rockall. Malin. Dogger. Finisterre.
(Carol Ann Duffy, b. 1955)[46]

'God's love is active in us so that our 'hidden self may grow strong' (Eph 3:16,19). Each self is a unique self, loved by God as a completely new creative experience, not as a member of any... 'ism'. The decision of the self to accept this, to let go (die) in trust is a new experience also for the Creator. It is our personal choice to respond or not to God and to one another. 'Come now, let us talk this over... says the Lord' (Is 10:17).

Eucharist/Thanksgiving/Celebrating Together
As part preparation for a meaningful celebration of the Eucharist, participants should be helped to focus upon God, who is forgiveness, mercy and unconditional love, and also on the Eucharistic Prayer and on the Eucharist itself.

All of creation is seen as a gift to us as we acknowledge a compassionate, forgiving, merciful God, rather than a God made unto our likeness, i.e. judgemental, vindictive, vengeful. We acknowledge a God who is Other, and we give praise and thanks.

The participants should try to see how they can more consciously be a part of God's plan. Can they be instruments of that plan to one another as they partake in this Eucharistic celebration? Can they be instruments of peace, of upbuilding? All of us are sinners and need to be liberated and restored. 'I came to call sinners' (Lk 5:30). In the presence of God we are beggars. The introduction of a tableau into the liturgy can help us comprehend a little better what it is to be a beggar or outcast, and understand the attitude of Francis and Clare to such outcasts. We can do that only by letting go of our prejudices and aversions, the things that sometimes we feel useless without. Through tableau or movement, expression can be given to insecurity, fear and defensiveness or to the feeling of being threatened.

The celebration of the Eucharist is central to the Christian tradition. It is a celebration of thanksgiving, to acknowledge the bounty and generosity of the Creator, in which all are meant to share. It should highlight the reality of our connectedness and our relationships in Christ. In the time of Francis and Clare, Eucharist was celebrated less often than it is now.

> whereas Francis' imagery for Christ was very Eucharistic, on the other hand, maybe it was because of the paucity of practice of the celebration of the Eucharist, that it was precious for Clare due to the infrequent reception of the sacrament among the poor ladies. According to Clare they were to receive the Eucharist seven times a year (Reg. Cl. 3:14).[47]

Everyone should participate in this Eucharistic celebration in a meaningful way. All should have that opportunity. All should seek to participate from the depths of the spirit. To make the participation more inclusive, suggestions for movements and gestures to express 'giving' should be gathered and accepted. Emphasis should be placed on the open hands as symbols of giving, of embracing and of healing.

> All we can hold in our cold, dead hands, is what we have given away.[48]

Henri Nouwen drew out the theme of Eucharist from the scriptural passage about the events on the road to Emmaus:

> But in the end, thanksgiving comes from above. In fact, our celebration of the Eucharist is a gift from above. It is the gift we cannot fabricate for ourselves; it is to be received. It is freely offered and asks to be freely received. That is where the choice is! We can choose to let the stranger continue his journey and so remain a stranger. We can also invite him into our inner lives, let him touch every part of our being, and transform our resentments into gratitude. We don't have to do this, in fact. Most people don't. But as often as we make that choice, everything, even the most trivial things, become new. Our little lives become great, part of the mysterious work of God's salvation. Once that happens, nothing is accidental, casual or futile any more. Eucharistic life, the life in which everything becomes a way of saying 'thank you' to him who joined us on the road.[49]

It is with burning hearts...

> There are many ways in which Jesus appears and many ways in which he lets us know that he is alive. What we celebrate in the Eucharist happens in many ways other than we might think. Jesus, who gave us bread already, touched the hearts of others long before he met us on the road.[50]

Have we stories to tell about significant encounters with people, particularly encounters that have somehow shown us that Christ is alive? These could be shared.

Eucharistic Living
1. List the consequences of hoarding.
2. How does greed originate? How does it grow, and why? What does trust in Providence mean? What might be the consequences of such trust in our lives?
3. What distinctions do we make between people in terms of status, importance, worth?

In contemplation and reflection, there is always the freedom to share what, in silence, the Lord has said. We enter into God's space to give Jesus space. We continually try to allow the initiative to be God's, to begin with the inspiration of Jesus who is 'the way'. We leave ourselves open to discovering the reality of Jesus, who is present in everyone, including our enemies. With his guidance and help we can grow to a fuller stature, closer to perfection.

Reflection on the bounty of God is essential and can be entered into at any time. God has given us the entire universe. It is we who put a price on it. A good exercise for the participants is to give a definition of generosity, bearing in mind the God who is totally generous, totally bountiful.

What do I find hardest to give? Each participant should ask for guidance in order to be able to acknowledge his or her own frailty. It can be an attachment to possessions, to a skill or talent, it can be an attachment to time. Today time is a prized commodity. Often we cannot give of our time. In all friendship, time is crucial. It is impossible to waste time in the company of God. Contemplation is effectively spending time with God, realising that in breathing in the creativity and bounty of God, we are breathing in life. We are often prepared to work *for* God, but not *with* God, and therefore, unlike Francis, we fail to appreciate our littleness, our nothingness. Participants should be encouraged to reflect on the presence of God who is always active, whether we are aware of it or not. God enjoys each individual's company, longs for it and loves it. For every stage of our journey, we need always to be linked to God, otherwise we can do nothing right.

Participants could talk about the ability to take time with God, and how this might help them grow in patience. Experiences might be recalled by the facilitator or the participants or both, which will help in understanding the wisdom of waiting on God, so that all will be encouraged to understand and appreciate that patience ultimately yields results.

Shared reflections will yield examples of how we are slaves to our own plans or those of other people, and how God can be curtailed to a certain slot in the day. God can be almost rendered irrelevant by our attitudes, but God's power can help us overcome our divisiveness in love. The more we allow God to be active, the more we will appreciate one another and all the blessings of the natural world. Divisions, and clinging to status, emerge too often from avarice and greed. We are afraid to let go and see ourselves and others as beloved children.

Consider what the artist achieves with stained glass. Every colour and every part has a place, and each part is seen as a beautiful part of the whole when the glass is held to the light. Consider our parts in the universe, that is, held up to the light, singular, unique and yet dependent, and all capable of amounting to one beautiful pattern.

Note the extent to which authority in our culture can depend upon subtle and not-so-subtle forms of bullying, through the power of money, strength of all kinds, and influence.

1. In a 'shame culture', what are the blockages that impede us from letting go of our prejudices?
2. How difficult is it for us to tell a story against ourselves?

Participants are free to comment and tell a story against themselves. Humorous incidents in life can be shared.

3. What reply can you give to the question: how does it feel to be perfect? How does it feel to be always right?

4. Recall some significant aspects of current lawsuits – hearts of stone? hearts of flesh? (Where an in-depth study is being made of this section of the process, significant aspects of current lawsuits might be gathered.)

The way chosen by Francis and Clare in their lives was one of peace and healing. In society today, what are the difficulties in achieving sisterhood/brotherhood? How can we begin to appreciate the sisterhood and brotherhood of all creation?

PEACE

Mahatma Gandhi once preached: 'Just as one must learn the art of killing in the training for violence, so one must learn the art of dying in the training for non-violence.'

Pope John Paul II said: 'Do not believe in violence; do not support violence. It is not the Christian way. Believe in peace and forgiveness and love; for they are of Christ.'[1]

> Peace was the mission of Francis: Francis' greeting to others, 'Peace be to you.' Holy Wisdom destroys Satan and all his subtlety.[2]

> Pure, holy Simplicity destroys all the wisdom of this world, and the wisdom of the body.[3]

> Holy Obedience destroys every wish of the body and of the flesh, and binds its mortified body to obedience of the Spirit, and to obedience of one's brother and [the person who possesses her] is subject and submissive to all persons in the world, and not to man only, but even to all beasts and wild animals, so that they may do whatever they want with him, inasmuch as it has been given to them from above by the Lord].[4]

KEY CONCEPTS
- Self for Others
- Our Mission
- Peace
- Reconciliation

Discussion 1
Share the gift of God. Relationship to another, poverty, service, liberation, Francis

> Finally, our soul becomes the likeness of the most blessed Trinity through righteous free will, only by manifesting robust virtue, pure truth, and ardent love; for robust virtue cleanses, strengthens, and elevates the soul, pure truth enlightens and reforms it and conforms it to God, ardent love perfects and vivifies it and unites it with God. When all of this is accomplished, (the person) is made pleasing and acceptable to God.[5]

> The world cannot always understand one's profession of faith, but it can understand service.[6]

> Spirituality is turning back to the Creator and becoming God-like by imitating Christ.[7]

> And Christ reveals who God is, and so shows us a self emptying love, that pours itself out in love for the other.[8]

> Ministers who are moved by an *imitatio Christi* that expresses itself in the desire to be a sign of God's loving action and incarnate presence are aware that their participation in the *missio Dei* – understood as God's universal loving will for all humanity – is not without its

risks and consequences. Grounded in this knowledge and experience, a theology of presence necessarily addresses itself not only to the mystery of God's love, but to the problem of God's love as well.[9]

Given the compassionate nature of God and God's presence, particularly in the weak and the oppressed, how can we discover that presence when our vision is so attracted to what is obvious, to what is strident, to what is powerful, to what distracts us, even in the name of charity, truth, obedience, poverty? How do we seek out the presence that is constantly creative: that does not injure the 'bruised reed'? How can we become instruments of peace rather than instruments of fear, manipulation or arrogance?

Using some of the quotations, participants can reflect on God's mission of peace and reconciliation to all of creation. Our support and promotion of human life must be accomplished through loving service. It must find expression in personal conviction first of all and then in witness, work, social activity and political commitment. This is particularly important now when *the culture of death* so forcefully opposes *the culture of life* and often seems to have the upper hand. However, regardless of circumstances, there is a need that springs from 'faith working through love' (Gal 5:6).[10]

Discussion 2
A celebration of the power of God as expressed in 'mercy' and 'forgiveness'

It would be useful for the participants to consider again Francis' and Clare's decisions, with perhaps examples from their lives, and some insight into the times in which Francis and Clare lived. It would help to recall the prayer 'Make Me an Instrument of Your Peace'. There is a need at this point for participants to experience a meaningful celebration of reconciliation. Reconciliation, in Franciscan spirituality, involves the whole of nature and at the same time involves a clear picture of the meaning of the death of Francis, the Transitus, and his stigmata at Laverna. Thus, reconciliation between all of creation and what that means needs to be celebrated. Celebration of the Transitus (death of Francis) will enrich this period if time permits.

Taking the Peace prayer, participants may share how anger can be healthily expressed in a way that diffuses frustration. In *doing the truth in love*, healing can come from the expression of personal hurt and disappointment, and at the same time leave room for the incongruities of human beings who are the cause of the hurt. At times, people's personal circumstances may seem impossible, which can make life very frustrating. We need to begin to trust in the providence of God, who is on our side. We need to trust in the basic goodness and lovability of humanity. Then we can provide for ourselves an inner serenity and security, knowing, like Francis, that the Lord is at the centre of our lives, and therefore 'the impossible' can be woven into the renewed fabric of our lives.

Discussion 3
How do we change hatred into love?
As we saw in Phase I, Humility, we start with our own lovableness. We can at least change the self-hatred of low self-esteem. We can seek to change that lack of charity towards others, which manifests itself as disgust, resentment, rash judgement or denigration, and that misunderstanding of God whereby we blame the divine for the faults and failures of the human condition. In so doing, we allow ourselves to be transformed.

We can constantly remind ourselves that we have been given the freedom to serve as instruments of healing, reconciliation and integration. The mission of God flows out of the desire to love. The divine response to humanity's need for redemption from sin is but one manifestation of that love.

The Franciscan mission of peace and charity is the unfolding of a reality given to us by Jesus Christ, but recognised and actualised by our own conversion to a free and open embracing of the gospel, by our risk-taking and honest commitment to justice, and by our self-giving service to one another. This peace and charity is both a promise and a pledge. It is God's gift and our task.[11] It is a calling to a different understanding of life, a call to another vision of living.

For Francis, following in the footsteps of Jesus was a new way of life, a risk, 'a vocation in terms of the generosity which inspired the response to the divine call and the constancy with which he followed it through'.[12] He was one with the marginalised so that he could always say that he was nothing but a beggar in need of help from everyone, and therefore, as he was no threat, he was a bringer of peace.

The search for true peace still goes on all over the world. Francis and Clare, following in the footsteps of the poor Christ, found and mirrored peace to their own and subsequent generations. They have left us that key to personal and universal peace.

Reflection 1
Lepers and leprosy
We find that, generally, the Church did try to hold out for the salvation of all, and therefore did, from time to time, point out the relationship between Jesus and the lepers. In the parable of Jairus and Lazarus, Lazarus was a leper at that time.

The idea of a leper as especially chosen by God for salvation was propagated primarily by the Church. According to a Latin chronicler (c. 1120-80), Louis VII spoke to lepers of Lazarus 'in order that they – burdened by infirmity of body – will study to deserve the health of their souls'.

215

My friend, it pleases our Lord that you should be infected with this disease, and our Lord gives you a great gift when He wishes to punish you for the evil you have done in this world. Wherefore have patience….

…this illness is the salvation of the soul, and that they ought not at all to say the truth.[13]

Following the First Crusade, when soldiers returned to Europe infected with leprosy, there was particular need for Christians to disassociate leprosy and sin.[14]

Therefore, 'leprosy indeed comes to be viewed as a sacred malady'.[15] Preachers taught about lepers and how Jesus himself would appear before the faithful in the form of a leper. However, it is important to remember that the older notion of leprosy as the disease prevailed, and that the notion that lepers were morally depraved produced effects more immediate and more enduring than those produced by the promise of divine grace. Again, if we remember Theodoric, the physician, he describes the leper as wrathful, malevolent and mistrustful – he suspects everyone wants to hurt him.

In the popular mind and in society at large, leprosy was a sinner's disease, associated with some abomination. Bible commentaries would refer to examples in the Bible to show that leprosy was a punishment for wickedness.

Therefore, this requires attention in order to fully appreciate Francis' conscious step to be among the outcast and marginalised so as to grasp the power and inclusiveness of the love of God[16] in the Incarnation.

Points to Ponder
- In the eyes of today's society, what is the 'sin' most deserving of punishment?
- What sins are ignored?
- What sins cause divisions among people, yet tend to be ignored as sins?
- How do we approach society, the world? – as profane; as secular; as sinful? Or as instruments of blessing; of peace – ready to receive a blessing and peace?

Reflection 2
Cruel to be kind
Francis became so ill in later life that he required the most bitter of medicines. As part of a medical procedure to restore his failing sight,

> his head was cauterised in several places, his veins opened, poultices applied, and drops poured into his eyes. Yet he had no improvement but kept getting steadily worse.[17]

In many ways, the whole of God's creation can appear hostile to us. For Francis, the hot poker on his eyes could have mirrored for him hostile elements in creation. But he 'addresses brother fire as if he were a person, asking him to be courteous to him in that hour'. The passage also reveals his astonishing will power.[18] By embracing the leper within himself, Francis made friends with all of creation.

Points to Ponder
- How is it possible for a foe to become a friend without any apparent alteration or transformation on the part of the foe?
- Can you give further examples?

Reflection 3
Creation – the sacrament of God
All of creation is full of the presence and the power of God. People who have pledged themselves to celibacy have made an act of trust in that presence and power and in the relationship that exists between all creation. They work for the reconciliation of all. So we give glory to God by appreciating all created things with our minds, hearts, wills and all our senses.

The decisions of Francis and Clare were made in the belief that they were walking in the footprints of Christ. Otherwise they could have no meaning.

Points to Ponder
• What might be the meaning of vows of chastity, poverty and obedience taken by people down through the centuries since the coming of Jesus Christ?

Reflection 4
Chastity
Chastity is related to simplicity, integrity, unity, so that there is neither division between who we are and who we say we are; between our deeds and our intentions. We celebrate reconciliation in order to open ourselves constantly to the possibility of growing in this unity through imitation of Christ.

Francis said:

> And all of us must keep close watch over ourselves and keep all parts of our body pure, since the Lord says: Anyone who looks lustfully at a woman has already committed adultery with her in his heart (Mt 5:28).[19]

and Paul says:

Do you not know that your members are the temples of the Holy Spirit? (cf. 1 Cor. 6:19); therefore, whoever violates God's temple, God will destroy him (1 Cor 3:17).[20]

Thus the whole of the body expresses itself as praise and communion within the heart of God and the universe.

In Francis' Later Rule:

> I also admonish and exhort these brothers that, in their preaching their words be well chosen and chaste (cf. Ps 11:7; 17:31), for the instruction and edification of the people, speaking to them of vices and virtues, punishment and glory in a discourse that is brief, because it was in few words that the Lord preached while on earth.[21]

Points to Ponder
- The sacrament of matrimony helps men and women to live chastely and fruitfully. Explain.
- Francis said we should be chaste in word. What does it mean to be chaste, chaste in deed, chaste in service?
- All of us are called to be chaste. What might that mean for us and for others?

Reflection 5
Hypocrisy
The innermost thoughts of the heart incline only to right action. Thus we seek all the time through our prayers, actions and thoughts to move from illusion to reality.

In the parable of the Pharisee and the publican, or tax-collector, (Lk 18:9-14), the Pharisee gives *himself* the credit for all his achievements. He talks in the first person: 'I'm not like others'; 'I fast'; 'I pay tithes from what income 'I possess'. He contrasts his virtue with that of the publican, who simply says, 'Be merciful to me, a sinner!' In his heart the Pharisee humiliates the publican and distances himself from the other worshippers in the temple. In so doing, he is not acknowledging his role as one of the people of God. He ignores and damages the notion of community.

We must acknowledge that all of us are hypocrites when we try to pray like the publican. And when we do this, it shows that in some way or another we regard ourselves as being closer to the publican than to the Pharisee. If we think we are closer to the publican than to the Pharisee, we are hypocritical in our prayer.

Points to Ponder
- Who are we when we are being hypocritical?
- What is happening?

Reflection 6
Christ shows us what it means to be human and reflects our future glory

> Having gazed longer into the mirror of Christ, in the crib and on the Cross, we ourselves become what Christ is, the unspotted mirror of wisdom reflecting the unimaginable glory of Jerusalem. Even we will taste that hidden sweetness which God has kept from the beginning, like a secret; we too will be kissed with the most joyful kiss of God's lips.[22]

Points to Ponder
- Describe ways in which we can best enter into the events of Jesus' life and death as described in the Gospels.

• Contemplate the account of the birth of Jesus. If possible, re-enact it in such a way that the helpless situation of a needy child and poor parents present clearly to the senses the word, the power and the glory made flesh in one moment of history. Try to discover in yourself in what circumstances and how you might be brought to your knees to adore such a phenomenon. 'Come let us adore Him.'

Reflection 7
The world

...a little thing, the size of a hazelnut, in the palm of my hand, and it was as round as a ball. I looked at it with my mind's eye and I thought, 'What could this be?' And the answer came, 'It is all that is made'. I marvelled that it could last, for I thought it might have crumbled to nothing, it was so small. And the answer came to my mind, It lasts and ever shall, because God loves it; and all things have being through the love of God. In this little thing I see three truths. The first is that God made it. The second is that God loves it. The third is that God looks after it. What is God indeed that is maker and lover and keeper? I cannot find words to tell. (Julian of Norwich, modernised from A Revelation of Love).

This is the hope against hope that our efforts on behalf of our planet are not ours alone, but that the source and power of life in the universe is working in and through us for the well-being of all creation, including our tiny bit of it.[23]

Another perspective is that of the contemporary novelist Alice Walker:

Helped are those who love the earth, their mother, and who willingly suffer that she may not die; in their grief over her pain they will weep rivers of blood, and in their joy in her lively response to love, they will converse with trees....

Helped are those who find the courage to do at least one small thing each day to help the existence of another – plant, animal, river, human being. They shall be joined by a multitude of the timid.

Helped are those who love and actively support the diversity of life; they shall be secure in their 'diversity'.

Helped are those who know.[24]

We are all called to become instruments of growth, of creativity, of reconciliation. God's approach is that of the artist. God lovingly works with creation, and we are invited to respond by the way we work and the time we take to understand God's ways.

Points to Ponder
•   Reflect on these insights and also consider the word 'instrument'.

Reflection 8
Mission – Desert as a way of life

The battle of the desert is waged, the courtship engaged, for no less a prize than where our true treasure will be stored up, and therefore where our hearts will be. The people of Israel were led through their geographic desert

3000 years ago, and, as a people, they have been through countless deserts since then. Moses, their long-suffering leader, went into the wilderness alone many times. So did Elijah, and other great Hebrew prophets. Also the great saints of Hinduism, Gautama, the Buddha and John the Baptist, and the Christian desert mothers and fathers and Mohammed, and so have countless pilgrims of all religions through the centuries. For modern pilgrims, the geographic desert often takes the form of temporary, silent solitude at a simple yet comfortable retreat centre or hermitage. For all, however, the desert of the heart remains unchanged. It is not comfortable.[25]

Points to Ponder
- My heart, God's heart – have they met?
- What might it mean if they did meet?
- What is prayer *now* for me?

Reflection 9
Deliverance... 'While I was still in sin, and after I tarried a while, I left the world' (Francis of Assisi)

Grace, thank God, can break through to us regardless of our intent. God graciously awaits our assent and our participation and transformation, but God does not wait to give us good things. No matter what our primary dedication may be at any given time, God's love can burst through upon us, miraculously. In my experience, these special miracles happen with uncommon frequency in the course of addictions. Without any evident reason, the weight of an addiction is lifted. 'I was walking to the grocery store one day,' said one alcoholic man, 'and there, on the sidewalk, I discovered equanimity.' He had suffered from alcoholism for many years, and that particular day had seemed no different from any other. Yet in a simple, wondrous moment, his life was transformed. He hasn't had a drink since. He did not describe his experience in religious terms. All he knew was that nothing he had learned, and nothing he had done, had made it happen.

This is the spiritual experience I learned about from recovering addicts, the unique phenomenon that sparked my professional-personal journey into psychology and spirituality. I can only call it deliverance. There is no physical, psychological, or social explanation for such sudden empowerment. People who have experienced them call them miraculous. In many cases these people have struggled with their addictions for years. Then suddenly, with no warning, the power of the addiction is broken. To me, deliverance is like any other miraculous physical, emotional, or social healing. It is an example of 'supernatural' or extraordinary 'grace', an obvious intervention by the hand of God in which physical structure and function are changed, and the growth towards wholeness is enabled. In the case of addiction, healing takes the form of empowerment that enables people to modify addictive behaviour.[26]

All grace is miraculous and yet, from the point of view of God, very natural. Francis came across this while working with lepers. It was when he disposed himself to the grace of God that God acted; and so what was bitter for him became sweet.

Points to Ponder
• Readers might call to mind incidents of this working of grace in ordinary, everyday events and in their own lives.

- Preparation for grace – is there such a thing?
- How might I prepare myself?

Reflection 10
Contemplation as a way of service, of reconciliation, of peace; daily practice

When trying to understand the idea of God's presence, being still and silent – whether saying a mantra or not – and doing nothing attentively, can be a means of allowing God to be active. This is contemplation. If I am unable to be still with my own company and enjoy it, how can I expect others to enjoy my company? My being still – doing nothing, thinking nothing, saying nothing – is a necessary exercise.

Points to Ponder
- Can we accept that God loves our company?
- Can we be still and keep company with God in such a way that we allow God to rejoice in our company?

Reflection 11
'Yes' to God

Gerald G. May, in his book *Addiction and Grace*, gives three examples of people who are addicted – one was a workaholic, the other sexually addicted, the other an alcoholic. In all of those cases, the people tried substitution, and yet there came a time when even that didn't work and they did not know which way to turn, so they just ceased being addicted – by their own decision. Gerald G. May would claim that when they stopped just because they had nowhere else to turn, and instead acknowledged their vulnerability, they portrayed a delicate spiritual quality. Their intent was simple; they maintained an open present-centredness. They ceased substituting addictions, like 'every time I feel like having a drink, I have a cup of coffee instead', 'any time I have sexual thoughts I'll put them out of my mind', or the busy executive, 'I make sure I meditate twenty minutes every day'.[27]

They allowed all the so-called props to fall away. They encountered spaciousness, and, to a degree, they made friends with it. They faced life 'in a truly undefended and open-eyed way'.[28]

> A contemplative quality can be found in anyone who has encountered emptiness and chosen not to run away. A sense of balance within spaciousness remains within such people, like a window between infinity and the world of everyday experience. They are not only wiser and humbler because of their addictions; they are also more available. Through their spaciousness, they are continually invited homeward. They have, in fact, already begun the homeward journey.[29]

To me, it is striking that their choices were so gentle, so plain. With everything I have said about the struggles of the desert, about resistances to asceticism, and about the power of consecration, one would expect such choices to be very dramatic. The yes that the heart speaks to God, we might assume, would be preceded by great intellectual considerations and emotional upheavals, and followed by enthusiastic celebration. Yet, in these stories, the yes was so quiet and so simple that it was barely noticed. Could it be that the heart speaks to God sometimes in ways that escape detection by our cellular representations? Is it possible that the heart can be in an act of consecration while the mind is still wondering what it's all about.

By the grace of God, the answer is yes. Of all the spiritual literature I have read, my favourite quotation is a simple one that was written by a very simple person.

Brother Lawrence, a seventeenth-century Carmelite friar, worked in the kitchen of his monastery and wrote a few words about practising the presence of God. Among those words are these: 'People would be surprised if they knew what the soul said to God sometimes'.[30]

Points to Ponder
- What are my particular addictions?
- What is my predominant weakness or addiction?
- What humiliates me, shames me, frightens me?
- What space have I given God to touch, heal and transform me?

Reflection 12
The soul's hunger – a sacred place

To be deprived of a simple object of attachment is to taste the deep, holy deprivation of our souls. To struggle to transcend any idol is to touch the sacred hunger God has given us. In such a light, what we have called asceticism is no longer a way of dealing with attachment, but an act of love. It is a willing, wanting, aching venture into the desert of our nature, loving the emptiness of that desert because of the sure knowledge that God's rain will fall, and the certainty that we are both heirs and co-Creators of the wonder that is now, and of the Eden that is yet to be.[31]

Points to Ponder
- How can we help one another to make the decisions that will enable us to take the straight and narrow path that leads to a true experience of ongoing wellbeing and joy of life?
- Is it possible?

- What are the most common obstacles to the journey of faith?
- What temptations might a Clare or Francis have encountered in the thirteenth century?

Reflection 13
World-view

> When religious beliefs lose touch with reality, they are likely to turn inwards and present a picture of the world which is no more than a mirror of ourselves, and such a mirror… is potentially dangerous. If our system of religious beliefs is to form a coherent world-view, as it did in the medieval model, it must look outwards to what contemporary science is telling us about the world around us.[32]

The reason many Christian doctrines are considered obsolete is that they are based on a very different picture of the world than the current one.

> It was a picture based largely on the physics and sociology of [Aristotle – fourth century BC] which was later elaborated into the medieval model…. In that picture, Heaven was completely separated from the earth… things in Heaven were not only made of a different substance from those on earth, but they obeyed different physical laws. Man and the earth were central to the whole scheme of things; Heaven was above [man's] head, and Hell was beneath his feet. Every detail of what man did and thought was closely watched over by God and his angels.[33]

In that kind of cosmology, divine intervention makes sense. However, it gives us the picture of a God from above who intervenes from outside the world and who is not part of it. Yet with Francis and Clare, the Incarnation was a decision of love. It was love in action, and this is what Francis imitated in embracing the leper, and similarly Clare when she embraced radical poverty. By the integrity of their life decisions, Francis and Clare embraced the whole world, so that the body, for both of them, was the action place of God – their cell, what in monastic terms would be called their cloister. In Francis' Canticle of the Creatures, all of creation is interrelated with the Creator and can only be understood in terms of that all-embracing connection.

Points to Ponder

- This understanding of connectedness grew with Francis through the years.
- How integrated am I? Do I feel I am one with myself, my body, other people, and with all of creation?

A passer-by complimented a farmer on his beautiful, well-tilled farm by saying: 'God and you have done a wonderful job on the farm'. The farmer replied: 'I would not like to see it if I left it to God'.

Even today, our conversation betrays our ability to leave God and the angels above our heads – outside. In God we move and have our being. God is the source of life. Without God – nothing.

Points to Ponder

- Our ability to disassociate the powerful presence of God from our lives and decisions is amazing. What does this say of the abuse of God's gift of love to us?

Reflection 14

The mysteriousness of beauty

Clare tells us that God is 'of such a beauty that the blessed hosts of Heaven never weary of admiring', of such love that we are stirred. She is telling us what she has learned herself, basing her certitude on her own experience, and this is what she tries to share with us. She knew it was more important to respond than to understand; she had learned that everything makes good sense even if it may not appear so. She knew that her part, like ours, was to be open, to receive and to respond to God, and to reflect upon God. In the process of learning such availability, she found that 'by such contemplation we are renewed/by such kindliness, flooded/by such gentleness, filled/gently enlightened by such a memory'. As a result, she is able and content to leave her limited understanding behind. All their lives, Francis and Clare worshipped beauty at its source, and this enabled them to recognise its reflections everywhere they looked. Even in their own lives, always notoriously difficult to judge, they knew the work of God when they saw it. 'The one who created you has made you holy,' Clare said encouragingly to herself as she lay dying, 'The one who created you has filled you with the Holy Spirit, and guarded you as a mother guards her child, he has loved you with a tender love'.[34]

Points to Ponder

- Peter's response to Jesus' question 'Will you also go away?' was: 'Where else do we go? You have the words of eternal life'. If this is our response also, what does it mean for us?
- Clare, Francis and Peter saw that Christ had the message of eternal life. In what ways do we look elsewhere for life, for fulfilment, for beauty?
- Why do we not believe in the way that Clare, Francis and Peter believed?

Reflection 15

Conversion. To serve, not to be served
The answer to Jesus' call to 'follow me' means serving others with compassion, grieving, forgiveness, generosity, reconciliation, becoming father, mother, brother, sister to all.

Points to Ponder
• What changes might have to take place in us if we were truly to follow Jesus' call?
• How do you view 'grace'?
• What vision have you now?
• What action will you now take, even in stages?
• Have you experienced any change of heart and mind?
• What do you understand by 'any change of heart and mind'?
• Would you foresee further changes of heart and mind in the future?
• As participants, what can we do from now on that will make a difference?
• What steps can we take – small but sure?
• What can *I* do – where do I go from here?
• Where do *we* go from here?

Reflection 16

The way of Christ – the way towards fulfilment
In following Christ, celibates exclude the possibility of marriage because they have discovered that the call to serve the kingdom makes them witnesses to God's open, generous love for all humanity.[35]

But Francis did not make the fatal mistake of believing that what was best for him personally had to be the best for everyone else, too. He did of course assist Clare and her companions to answer God's call to virginal chastity. He understood that chastity is a grace that is necessary for spreading the kingdom on earth; but whether to do so from the celibate state or from the state of married chastity was a decision for each person to make according to the gift he or she received from God.[36]

Points to Ponder

- What does your understanding of the life of Jesus evoke in you?
- What is life with Christ for you?
- Assess what it could be like to be a follower of Christ.
- What is death for you?
- What is life for you, both positively and negatively?

Reflection 17

To persevere on our journey

Prayer of Clare to Agnes of Prague

'What you hold, may you [always] hold.
What you do, may you [always] do, and never abandon,
  But with swift pace, light step,
  [and] unswerving feet,
  so that even your steps stir up no dust,
go forward
  securely, joyfully, and swiftly
  on the path of prudent happiness.[37]

Points to Ponder

- Translate this prayer in practical terms for the present, as it relates to yourselves as a group and/or to yourself as an individual.

Reflection 18
A way that disturbs

The way of Gospel life which Francis took was subversive even though he did not intend it to be, and it was subversive because it clashed with the new values which the society of his day was evolving. People's first reaction to him was to say that he was crazy, and to push him aside, because they could not tolerate anyone who thought and lived like a truly free man. They looked upon such an attitude as dangerous, and it made them feel uneasy.[38]

Points to Ponder
• The 'two-edged' sword – when we receive the word what happens?
• Does the word become flesh in us?
• If not, why not? What are the obstacles?

Reflection 19
The risk taken – faith and glory

PRAISE: Glory to God

1. Will you come and follow me
if I but call your name?
Will you go where you don't know
and never be the same?
Will you let my love be shown,
will you let my name be known,
will you let my life be grown
in you and you in me?

2. Will you leave yourself behind
if I but call your name?

Will you care for cruel and kind
and never be the same?
Will you risk the hostile stare?
should your life attract or scare?
Will you let me answer prayer
in you and you in me?

3. Will you let the blinded see
if I but call your name?
Will you set the prisoners free
and never be the same?
Will you kiss the leper clean,
and do such as this unseen,
and admit to what I mean
in you and you in me?

4. Will you love the 'you' you hide
if I but call your name?
Will you quell the fear inside
and never be the same?
Will you use the faith you've found
to reshape the world around
through my sight and touch and sound
in you and you in me?

5. Lord, your summons echoes true
when you but call my name.
Let me turn and follow you
and never be the same.
In your company I'll go
where your love and footsteps show.
Thus I'll move and live and grow
in you and you in me.[39]

Points to Ponder
- Meditate and share your thoughts on the words and theme of this hymn.

Reflection 20
From alienation to unity

We need to recover our sense of relatedness to all of creation. We need to hope for transformations/resurrection for all of creation. The Creator does not intend anything for the wastepaper basket. God does not create trash.

Lester Brown, president of the Worldwatch Institute, reports:

> As we approach the new millennium, there are growing signs that the world may be on the edge of an environmental revolution comparable to the political revolution that swept Eastern Europe,

> ...For many who track environmental trends, such as collapsing fisheries, shrinking forests, rising temperatures, and the wholesale loss of plant and animal species, it has been clear for some time that economic progress can be sustained only if the economy is restructured so that its natural support systems can be protected.

> For those not already convinced of the need to replace the Western, fossil-fuel-based, automobile-centred, throwaway economy with an economy that would be environmentally sustainable, what is happening as China modernises offers compelling new evidence. For example, a car in every garage in China, American style, would not only deprive China of scarce cropland, but would also drive China's oil consumption to some 80 million barrels a day, well above the current world production of 67 million barrels per day.

If the western industrial development model will not work for China, it will not work for India, whose population will reach 1 billion later this year, or for the other 2 billion people in the developing world.... And in an integrated global economy, it will not work over the long term for the industrial countries either.[40]

Brown argues that there is an exciting alternative economic model that promises a better life everywhere without destroying the earth's natural support systems. The new economy will be powered not by fossil fuels, but by various sources of solar energy and hydrogen. Urban transportation systems will be centred not around the car, but around high-tech light-rail systems augmented by bicycles and walking. Instead of a throwaway economy, we will have a reuse/recycle economy.

Increased pressures on the world environment
- Population increasing by 96 million per year
- 50 percent live in cities
- 800 million live in absolute poverty
- Every hour 1,500 children die of hunger
- Every minute US$1.8 million is spent on defence
- 80 percent of natural resources are used by 25 percent of the population
- 20 percent of the world's population lacks access to clean water[41]

Increased Pressures on the Irish Environment
- Increased road traffic
- Intensification of agriculture
- Increased solid waste generation
- More rivers and lakes 'moderately polluted'
- 18 percent of flora and fauna threatened

- Overgrazing of hill land
- Collapse of sea trout fisheries[42]

The World's Priorities (Annual Expenditure)
- Basic education for all   £4.0B
- Cosmetics in the USA   £5.5B
- Water and sanitation for all   £6.0B
- Ice-cream in Europe   £8.0B
- Women's reproductive health   £8.0B
- Perfumes in Europe and USA   £8.0B
- Basic health and nutrition   £9.0B
- Pet foods in Europe and USA   £12.0B
- Cigarettes in Europe   £34.5B
- Alcoholic drinks in Europe   £72.0B
- World narcotic drugs   £276.0B
- World military spending   £538.0B[43]

The three richest people are wealthier than the poorest forty-eight countries.

Points to Ponder
- What might be the results of an economy based on the politics of compassion and an attitude of caring for creation?

Reflection 21
Values
All of creation, with its variety of gifts and treasures, can be focused upon by an individual or group through the lens of a predominant value, such as power, authority or money. Only the light of the Creator enhances the uniqueness and worth of every individual item of creation. Only the light of the Creator makes of each individual man and woman the king, queen,

spokesperson and guardian of all creation. To acknowledge the Creator and our creaturehood is to enhance the value of all of creation, so that all of creation deserves our respect and reverence because of its relatedness to the Creator. To choose to live by any other value system is to diminish and enslave creation to a very limited value.

> If you were to say to the grown-ups: 'I saw a beautiful house made of rosy brick, with geraniums in the windows and doves on the roof,' they would not be able to get any idea of that house at all. You would have to say to them: 'I saw a house that cost $200,000.' Then they would exclaim: 'Oh, what a pretty house that is!'[44]

> There are different companies – the stronger, the handsome, the intelligent, the devout – and each man reigns in his own, not elsewhere. But sometimes they meet, and the strong and the handsome fight for mastery – foolishly, for their mastery is of different kinds. They misunderstand one another, and make the mistake of each aiming at universal dominion. Nothing can win this, not even strength, for it is powerless in the kingdom of the wise.[45]

Art can become a money thing. Constantine used Christianity as an instrument of government. Friendship can be used out of ambition – a prostitution of real values.

> Man, who discovers his capacity to transform and in a certain sense create through his own work, forgets that this is always based on God's prior and original gift of the things that are. Man thinks that he can make arbitrary use of the earth, subjecting it without restraint to his will, as

though it did not have its own requisites and a prior God-given purpose, which man must indeed develop but must not betray.... In all this, one notes first the poverty or narrowness of man's outlook, motivated as he is by a desire to possess things rather than to relate them to the truth, and lacking that disinterested, unselfish and aesthetic attitude that is born of wonder in the presence of being and of the beauty which enables one to see in visible things the message of the visible God who created them.[46]

We are not yet in a position to assess the biological disturbance that could result from indiscriminate genetic manipulation and from unscrupulous development of new forms of plant and animal life, to say nothing of unacceptable experimentation regarding the origins of human life itself. It is evident to all that in any area as delicate as this, indifference to fundamental ethical norms or their rejection would lead mankind to the very threshold of self-destruction.[47]

We can help one another to let go, to tear away from the values 'of the world'. We cannot over emphasise the importance of discerning the values by which we live. Are they gospel values? So we repeat: we need again to look at values: our values.

These 'values' can put pressure on us to seek fame at any cost. They can put pressure on us to value our contribution only in terms of money instead of giving time to husband, wife, children, friends, people in need. People can be used as commodities, whether it be as sex objects or status objects. Sexual gratification can become the principal goal of human relationships. Groups of people who do not think or act as we do can be dismissed. Injustices that give rise to resentments can be ignored.

Points to Ponder
If offered, which would I choose:
- wisdom;
- peace;
- money now;
- friendship with God?

Reflection 22
Contemporary expressions of Franciscan peace

Peace Prayer
Lord, make me an instrument of your peace:
Where there is hatred, let me sow love.
Where there is discord, harmony.
Where there is injury, pardon.
Where there is error, truth.
Where there is doubt, faith.
Where there is despair, hope.
Where there is darkness, light.
Where there is sadness, joy.
Oh, Divine Master! Grant that I may not so much seek to
be consoled, as to console;
to be understood, as to understand;
to be loved, as to love.
For it is in giving that we receive
[it is in forgetting self that we find ourselves];
it is in pardoning that we are pardoned;
it is in dying that we are born to eternal life.

Though only one hundred years old, this prayer still expresses accurately the spirit of St Francis, which has been handed down in tradition.

The anonymous author of the prayer for peace seems to have drawn his inspiration from the sources of piety that were familiar at the time. His poetic gifts and inner conviction enabled him to elevate his sources to the moving simplicity of a little masterpiece, whose success continues to demonstrate its perennial worth.[48]

Points to Ponder

- Can we make a peace prayer for today's world using this Peace Prayer as a model?
- Can we in our prayer include problems of justice and peace, and also the ecological issues that derive from our inhumanity to other people and to all of creation?

Reflection 23

Francis – instrument of peace

After Blessed Francis had composed the Praises of the Creatures, which he called The Song of Brother Sun, a serious dispute happened to arise between the Bishop of Assisi and the mayor. As a result, the bishop excommunicated the mayor, and the mayor issued an order forbidding anyone to sell anything to the bishop, to buy anything from him, or to make any agreement with him.

Although Blessed Francis was ill when he heard of this, he was deeply grieved on their account, especially as there was no one to make peace between them. And he said to his companions, 'It brings great disgrace on us when the bishop and mayor hate one another in this way, and no one can make peace between them'. So he immediately wrote a verse to be included in the Praises for this occasion, and said:

Praise to Thee, my Lord, for those who pardon one
another
For Love of Thee, and endure
Sickness and tribulation;
Blessed are they who shall endure it in peace,
For they shall be crowned by Thee,
O Most High.[49]

Reflection 24
Relationship of creator/creature – a hymn of praise

Canticle of the Creatures
Most High, all-powerful, good Lord,
Yours are the praises, the glory, the honour, and the blessing.
To You alone, Most High, do they belong
and no one is worthy to mention Your name.

Praised be You, my Lord, with all Your creatures
especially Sir Brother Sun
Who is the day and through whom You give us light
And he is beautiful and radiant with great splendour
and bears a likeness of You, Most High One.
Praised be You, my Lord, through Sister Moon and the stars,
in heaven You formed them clear and precious and
beautiful.

Praised be You, my Lord, through Brother Wind,
and through the air, cloudy and serene, and every kind of
weather
through which You give sustenance to Your creatures.
Praised be You, my Lord, through Sister Water,
who is very useful and humble and precious and chaste.

Praised be You, my Lord, through Brother Fire,
through which you light the night
and he is beautiful and playful and robust and strong.

Praised be You, my Lord, through our Sister Mother Earth,
who sustains and governs us,
and who produces various fruits with coloured flowers and
herbs.

Praised be You, my Lord, through those who give pardon
for Your love,
and bear infirmity and tribulation.
Blessed by those who endure in peace
for by You, Most High, shall they be crowned.

Praised be You, my Lord, through our Sister Bodily Death,
from whom no one living can escape.
Woe to those who die in mortal sin,
Blessed are those whom death will find in Your most holy
will,
for the second death shall do them no harm.
Praise and bless my Lord and give him thanks
and serve him with great humility.[50]
(St Francis of Assisi)

G. K. Chesterton once wrote that this canticle 'is a
supremely characteristic work and much of Saint Francis
could be reconstructed from that work alone.' (Chesterton
1924, 132). Some might dismiss that sweeping statement
of the English editorialist on the grounds that he was not
as cognisant of Francis' writings as we are now. Yet Eloi
Leclerc, a contemporary French author, resonates with
Chesterton's observation: 'The manner in which Francis

here looks at the created world is a key to his inner self, for the canticle undoubtedly has elements that reveal in a special way the personality of its author.' (Leclerc 1978, 4). In order to appreciate the insights of both Chesterton and Leclerc, we must look carefully not only at the canticle's structure, the frequent practice of commentators, but also at the very words Francis uses in his praises.[51]

Francis envisions us, human beings, taking our rightful place in the hymn of praise, for we share with God that awesome power of granting pardon because of love. Yet he realises that we are incapable of being reconcilers or peacemakers unless we assume the attitudes of the Suffering Servant of God, Jesus, who so forcefully reveals the mysterious ways of God. We find ourselves recalling the admonitions and especially those that commented on the beatitude of the peacemaker, the thirteenth and fifteenth admonitions. Or we find ourselves reflecting upon the ways of the Spirit, as Francis describes them in chapter 17 of the Earlier Rule; there he tells us that one who follows these ways 'strives for humility and patience, and the pure, simple and true peace of the Spirit'. Thus the 'Canticle of Unity', in which we had no place, now becomes a 'Canticle of Reconciliation', in which those who have identified with Jesus have their rightful place.[52]

The death of the body is no longer something to be feared or dreaded, Francis sings. Now it is a sister, an instrument of God's presence, to be welcomed and embraced. When Sister Bodily Death finds us doing God's will, the last judgement will not harm us. It was as if Francis knew that everything he had tasted of in this world was only a foretaste of what was to come. This explains his sorrow for those who died in mortal sin and his conviction that those whose concern is simply God's will are blessed.

> Francis' last words were, then, the refrain of his 'Canticle of the Creatures'. As Sister Bodily Death met the Lord's servant, naked as when he entered the world, he sang ever so poignantly and left us, in all its simplicity, a reflection of his entire life.[53]

Francis dramatically requested that he die naked. It was an expression of the desire that should always permeate our hearts – to be naked before God. In God we trust. The vision of a freedom of the children of God, with no desire to cover up our nakedness, no guilt feelings, no feelings of being threatened, absence of desire to justify oneself, the acceptance of one another and the unique and important role each has to play, should facilitate us on our return journey to a land where all belong, where everything is held in common, and where each has enough. The generous Garden of Eden is loving asceticism transformed into bountifulness unlimited. It is the glory of the resurrection initiated by Christ and us here and now. It can get a kick-start from some events in our lives that profoundly change our direction or it can be a process on a pathway lit continually by the life and truth of Christ.

EPILOGUE

This process or journey is one way of helping ourselves both as individuals and as a community to discover the pathway to life. As individuals, it helps us bring our dreams, disappointments, ambitions, failures, hurts, sins, joys to God. Our tensions will be resolved only in encounter with the Creator. We are invited to work as sisters and brothers with Christ, not for him. We are gifts given to each other – not threats. 'The Spirit wakes all people, free people, ready to put aside self-love, integrate earthly resources into human life, and reach out to the future when humanity itself will become an offering accepted by God'.[1] The new humanity will be one which Christ has raised up in the world through his Spirit.

The Spirit gives us our identity when we choose to let go and discover our hidden treasure. By discovering and acknowledging this Spirit in my 'enemy', I not only acknowledge the universal parenthood of God, but I also acknowledge the intense bond of love that exists between every human being in his or her uniqueness with his or her Creator. 'All aesthetic experience is feeling arising out of the realisation of contrast under identity.'[2]

This is the source of a religious experience. This bond for a human being is not without feeling. The use of the idea of motherhood by both Francis and Clare means that the Creator-creature bond is not meant to be without feelings, tears, and emotions – otherwise it is not real. Human compassion devoid of feeling and empathy is not compassion. Eternal joy is eternal growth, newness, without illusions. The more one resembles the compassionate humanity of Christ, the more one becomes truly human, or, for Francis and Clare, the more one became truly holy.

A certain growth also remains possible in the final fulfilment. Otherwise we would perhaps cease to be human. Just as life constantly rediscovers itself from the past into the future, so we shall constantly rediscover our past and present in and from God in new and surprising ways.[3]

In one of his spiritual conferences, a Capuchin Franciscan says: 'only compassionate love glowing in the heart will urge one to comfort the sorrowing Christ – no arguments of the mind no matter how convincing'.[4]

Christ grieves in *his persecuted body* 'we know that all [the persecuted body] of creation is groaning in labour pains until now' (Rom 8:22). 'We who have the first fruits groan within ourselves as we await for adoption' (Rom 8:23). To those who diligently wanted to journey along the pathway discovered by Francis, he said: '...as pilgrims and strangers (cf. 1 Pet 2:11) in his world who serve the Lord in poverty and humility, let them go begging for alms with full trust'.[5]

Christ has made us his sisters and brothers, his trust in human beings has been vindicated, and our acceptance of Mary as our mother can only be actualised in our corresponding trust in human beings. The great scandal of the church of Christ and of those who call themselves followers of Christ is to despise 'the despised'. That is the way of the world.

Even in Old Testament times, Ham, in exposing the drunken nakedness of his father to his brothers Shem and Japheth, was deemed to imply contempt for his father and his plight. Shem and Japheth respectfully went back into the tent (to avoid looking on their father) and covered him with a cloak. Ham, the father of Canaan, was subsequently cursed by Noah when he heard what happened. 'Cursed be Canaan, the lowest of slaves shall he be to his brothers' (Gen 9:18-25). Is our tendency to 'expose' people today a quest for truth or have we taken a pathway that leads deeper into the night – a pathway that exploits the vulnerability of others for money, for vengeance, out of envy or jealousy? In the western world, is this the choice of death, is this the ultimate in playing God?

The Creator has chosen to suffer the rejections, the struggles and the frustrations of creation. God loves creation, loves the world and expresses this love by respecting its autonomy. For human beings, love is also expressed by the Creator in respecting our freedom – our freedom to choose and to accept the path to death or the path to life.

> There is a certain amount of suffering, misunderstanding, and existential absurdity that is inherent in human life, as we all know. Each of us passes through crises that offer us the chance to grow or that may become enormous traumas. All humans must resolve their Oedipus complex, that is to say, attain their autonomy and be their own person, something that becomes a fine drama for some and a tragedy for others. No one can spend one's entire life avoiding the great question of personal death, neglecting to define oneself in terms of the meaning of human hope. To treat these questions is more than to elaborate some theory that is then simply forgotten. It means to build a path that must be travelled day by day, without illusions and with a sober resignation (ataraxia) that is the expression of the wisdom of an adult spirit.[6]

The future of the world to which Christians look in hope is a future which, even though it is worked out in history, will find its ultimate fulfilment in a state that transcends our historical experience. It will be that final state of existence with God in which the creative power of God's self-giving love will totally suffuse all creaturely relations, transforming all into the final perfection of love and mutuality. And 'God will be all in all' (1 Cor 15, 18).[7]

Bearing in mind the above quotations, what are the beacons and the lights that guide us on our way through the shadows of our everyday living to the substance of eternal light and life?

And this, after all, means that he achieved exactly what in the first place he set out to do: he preached his life, which is the best way, the most effective Christian sermon that has ever been preached: a sermon which still, after all the centuries, works its gentle ferment and attains its design, because if in reading it we learn to love Francis, we must find ourselves loving also his Master and his Model.[8]

Let us, as a group, bless each other from our hearts as Paul blessed the Thessalonians: 'May the God of Peace make you whole and holy; and may you all be kept safe and blameless in spirit, soul and body for the coming of our Lord Jesus Christ' (1 Thess 23).

ABBREVIATIONS

Abbreviations for quotations taken from Franciscan sources:

Adm   The Admonitions
CtC   The Canticle of the Creatures
RNB   The Earlier Rule (Regula non bullata – not officially
        approved by the Holy See)
RB   The Later Rule (Regula bullata – approved by the
        Holy See)
Test   The Testament
1 Cel   The Life of St Francis by Thomas of Celano
2 Cel   Celano's second Life of St Francis
L3C   The Legend of the Three Companions
LM   Major Life of St Francis by St Bonaventure
Lm   Minor Life of St Francis by St Bonaventure

NOTES

Introduction

1 Stanley Hauerwas, *The Peaceable Kingdom* (Notre Dame: University of Notre Dame Press, 1983), p. 29.

2 Marian A. Habig, ed., *St Francis of Assisi: Writings and Early Biographies, English Omnibus of the Sources for the Life of St Francis* (Quincy, IL: Franciscan Press, 1972), 2 Cel 95, p. 441.

3 Ibid., 2 Cel 214, p. 534; LM XIV 3, p. 739.

4 Ibid., RB 10:8.

5 Ibid., LM XIV 3.

6 Regis Armstrong OFMCap and Ignatius C. Brady OFMCap, *Francis and Clare: The Complete Works* (New York: Paulist Press, 1982), p. 154, 1-3.

7 Ibid., RNB XVI, pp. 121-2.

Francis of Assisi

1. Regis J. Armstrong OFMCap, J. A. Wayne Hellman OFM, William J. Short OFM, *Francis of Assisi: Early Documents*, vol. 1, *The Saint* (New York: New City Press, 1999), ch. VI, pp. 193-4.

2 Habig, *Omnibus of Sources*, 'Legend of the Three Companions', ch. VI, 19, 20, pp. 908-9.

3 Pope Gregory IX who, as Cardinal Hugolino, helped Francis personally, speaking on 19 July 1228, two years after Francis' burial and three days after his canonisation.

Clare of Assisi

1 Regis J. Armstrong OFMCap, *Clare of Assisi: Early Documents*, First Letter to Agnes 30 (New York: Franciscan Institute Publications, 1993), pp. 37-8.

2 Ibid., First Letter to Agnes of Prague, 19, 20, 21, p. 37.

3 Mary Frances Hone, ed., *Clare's Form of Life*, The Clare Centenary Series, Franciscan Process 12 (Franciscan Institute Publications), p. 72.

4 Armstrong and Brady, *Francis and Clare*, 20, p. 204.

5 Hone, *Clare's Form of Life*, vol. III, Process 1, 2.

Preliminaries for Understanding Franciscan (Creation) Spirituality

1   Teresa of Avila, Interior Castle, 54.

2   Habig, *Omnibus of Sources,* LM, ch. VI, p. 671.

3   Thomas Merton, *Conjectures of a Guilty Bystander,* p. 158.

4   Timothy Ware, ed., 'Theophane, the Recluse' in *The Art of Prayer: An Orthodox Anthology* (London: Faber & Faber, 1971), p. 191.

5   St Francis de Sales, *Treatise on the Love of God,* AEX: 270-71 (Rockfort, IL: Tan Books, 1995).

6   Habig, *Omnibus of Sources,* RNB, 22-29.

7   André Cirino OFM, *Franciscan Solitude* (New York: Josef Raischi Institute, St Bonaventures, 1995), p. 118-19.

8   Apophthegmata Patrum De. Abbote Joanne Colobol, pp. 65-203.

9   R. S. Thomas, *Collective Poems 1945-1990* (London: J. M. Dent, 1993).

10   *The Complete Works of Oscar Wilde* (London: Chancellor Press, 1991), p. 854.

11   Armstrong/Hellman/Short, *Francis of Assisi: Early Documents,* ch. VI, 103, p. 273.

Phase I – Humility

1   Evans, Donald, *Struggle and Fulfilment* (Philadelphia: Fortress Press, 1979), pp. 111-12.

2   *Gaudium et Spes,* ed. A. Flannery, p. 915.

3   Armstrong and Brady, *Francis and Clare,* Clare, Testament 7, p. 228.

4   Malcolm Muggeridge and Alec Vidler, *Paul: Envoy Extraordinary,* (London: Collins, 1972), pp. 46-8.

5   Viktor E. Frankl, *Man's Search for Meaning* (New York: Pocket Books, 1963), p. 213.

6   Francis Baur OFM, *Life in Abundance* (New York: Paulist Press, 1983), p. 161.

7   Duane Beane, 'Prison is House of Mirrors, Reflecting the Inner Self', from NukeWatches, *Prisoners on Purpose: A Peacemaker's Guide to Jails and Prisons* (reprinted *National Catholic Reporter,* 29 December 1989), p. 2.

8   United States Catholic Conference, *Catechism of the Catholic Church* (Ligouri Publications, 1994), 2558, p. 613.

9   Ibid., 2560, p. 614.

10 Ibid.

11 G. K. Chesterton, *Saint Francis of Assisi* (New York: Doubleday, 1957), p. 73.

12 Armstrong and Brady, *Francis and Clare*, The Earlier Rule NB, p. 128.

13 Henri Nouwen, *The Return of the Prodigal Son* (New York: Image Books, Doubleday, 1998), p. 121.

14 Armstrong and Brady, *Francis and Clare*, Testament, pp. 154-6.

15 John Vanier, *Be Not Afraid* (Toronto: Griffin House, 1975), p. 28.

16 Armstrong and Brady, *Francis and Clare*, Admonition, 7, 3-4, p. 30.

Phase II – Sisterhood and Brotherhood

1   Jean Vanier, 'Understanding Our Own Business' in *Spiritual Journeys*, ed. Stanislaus Kennedy RSC (Dublin: Veritas, 1997).

2   Leonardo Boff, *St Francis* (London; SCM Press, 1982), 2 Cel 146, p. 122.

3   Michael Blastic OFMConv, *Clare of Assisi: The Eucharist and John 13*, in Clare Centenary Series: Clare of Assisi Investigations, vol. 7 (New York: Franciscan Institute Publications, 1953), p. 39.

4   J. O'Donoghue, *Anam Cara: A Book of Celtic Wisdom* (New York: Harper Collins, 1997), p. 63.

5   Armstrong and Brady, *Francis and Clare*, The Earlier Rule, p. 116.

6   Ibid., Admonition, 2, p. 27.

7   G. K. Chesterton, *St Francis of Assisi*, p. 79.

8   David Peterson, *Possessed by God: A New Testament Theology of Sanctification and Holiness* (Grand Rapids, MI: Eerdmans, 1995), p. 106.

9   Ignatius Kelly OFM, 'Poverty as a Spiritual Value', *The Way*, Supplement 80 (1994), pp. 25-32.

10 G. K. Chesterton, *St Francis of Assisi*, p. 80.

11 Habig, *Omnibus of Sources*, Major Life, ch. 2, no. 6, p. 644.

12 Armstrong and Brady, *Francis and Clare*, Second Letter to Agnes, 19, p. 197.

13 Richard Palmer, 'The Church, Leprosy and Plague', in *Studies in Church History*, vol. 19 (Oxford: Blackwell 1982), p. 80.

14 Dorothy Day, *Loaves and Fishes* (Maryknoll, New York: Orbis Books, 1997), p. 74.

15 Luciano Canonici, 'Leper, Leprosarium', *Greyfriars Review*, vol. 9, no. 3 (1995), p. 257.

16 Ibid.

17 Jacques Rossland, *Medieval Prostitution* (Cambridge, MA: Blackwell), pp. 57-9.

18 Arnoldo Fortini, *Nova Vita II:* 257-61 (1980), p. 265.

19 Hermann Schaluck OFM, 'Evangelization: From Tradition to Prophecy – To Fill the Whole Earth with the Gospel of Christ' (Saint Louis: English Speaking Conference, 1996).

20 Armstrong and Brady, *Francis and Clare*, The Later Rule, ch. 10, Reg. 7 and 8, pp. 143-4.

21 Ibid., ch. 6, RB., p. 141.

22 Ibid., Third Letter to Agnes, 2, p. 199.

23 J. F. Godet, 'Progetto Evangelico de Chiaro Oggi', *Vita Minorum* 56 (1985), p. 240.

24 Armstrong and Brady, *Francis and Clare*, p. 28.

25 Helmut Gollwitzer, *The Way to Life: Sermons in a Time of World Crisis* (Edinburgh: T&T Clark, 1981), p. 152.

26 Armstrong and Brady, *Francis and Clare*, ch. 9, p. 117.

27 G. K. Chesterton, *Saint Francis of Assisi*, pp. 68-70.

28 *The Intellectuals*, p. 4.

29 Christopher Martin, *Trespass Against Francis* (Great Wakering: Mayhew/McCrimmon, 1979), p. 52.

30 Adrian Van Kaam, *Personality Fulfilment in the Religious Life* (Wilkes-Barre, PA: Dimension Books, 1967).

31 Second Letter of the Conference of the Franciscan Family on the Occasion of the Jubilee 2000 in the Year of the Holy Spirit, no. 14.

32. Julian of Norwich, from Anthony P. Castle, ed., *Quotes and Anecdotes for Preachers and Teachers* (Kevin Mayhem Publishers, 1979).

Phase III – Peace

1   P. Benoit OP, 'L'Ascension', *Exegese et theologie* 1 (Paris, 1961), p. 386.

2   Yves Congar OP, *The Mystery of the Church* (London: Geoffrey Chapman, 1965), p. 172.

3   Arturo Paoli, *Meditations on Saint Luke* (Maryknoll), p. 6.

4   Billy Graham, *Just As I Am* (London: Harper Collins, 1997).

5   Armstrong and Brady, *Francis and Clare*, Admonitions, pp. 26-7.

6   Ibid., Letter to the Entire Order, 26-29, p. 58.

7   Zachary Hayes OFM, 'Christ, Word of God and Exemplar of Humanity: The Roots of Franciscan Christocentrism and Identification Today', *The Cord*, Vol. 46, 1, (1996), p. 16.

8   Armstrong/Hellman/Short, *Francis of Assisi*, Celano 85, p. 255.

9   E. Cousins, 'Francis of Assisi, Christian Mysticism at the Crossroads', in *Mysticism and Religious Traditions*, ed. Stephen Katz (Oxford University Press, 1979), pp. 163-90, and especially pp. 166-9.

10 William R. Cook, *Francis of Assisi* (MGP, Liturgical Press, 1989), pp. 88-9.

11 *Carolau Plygain/Plygain Carols*, trans. Geraint Vaughan Jones (Welsh Folk Museum, 1977), p. 450. Taken from *Doctrine and Life*, vol. 35 (October 1985), article by Mr Harri Pritchard Jones 'The Welsh Catholic Tradition', pp. 446-56.

12 Luciano Canonici, 'Leper, Leprosarium', *Greyfriars Review*, vol. 9, no. 3 (1995), p. 252.

13 Octavian Schmucki OFM, 'Initiation into the Franciscan Life: Early Sources', *Greyfriars Review*, vol. 2 (June 1998), p. 7.

14 Helmut Gollwitzer, *The Way to Life* (Edinburgh: T&T Clark), p. 114.

15 Margaret Guider, 'Foundation for a Theology of Presence: A Consideration of the Scotist Understanding of the Primary Purpose of the Incarnation, and Its Relevance for Ministry, in the Underworld and the World Church', *The Cord*, vol. 43, no. 3 (March 1993), p. 75.

16 Benet A. Fonck, *Fully Mature with the Fullness of Christ*, Third Edition (Franciscan Province of the Sacred Heart), ch. 7, ch. 39.

17   Robert Sardello, 'Working with the Guardian Angels' in *The Angels* (New York: Continuum), p. 208.
18   Thomas Henry Huxley, *What Great Men Think of Religion*.
19   John Foster Dulles.
20   *In Conversation with Elie Wiesel* (New York, 1976), p. 3.
21   H. Paul Santmire, *The Travail of Nature: The Ambiguous Promise of Christian Theology* (Minneapolis: Fortress Press, 1985), p. 178.
22   *The Body of God: An Ecological Theology* (Minneapolis: Fortress Press, 1993), p. 110.
23   Arthur Mizener, ed., *Modern Short Stories*, revised edition (New York: W. Norton and Co.) pp. 137-49.
24   Billy Graham, *Just As I Am* (London: Harper Collins, 1997).
25   Habig, *Omnibus of Sources*, L3C, 36:58-60.

Resources: Humility
1   Armstrong and Brady, 'Salutation of the Virtues', in *Francis and Clare* (Paulist Press), pp. 151-2.
2   Vinje, Patricia M., 'An Understanding of Humility in St Teresa's Interior Castle', *Review for Religious* (Jan-Feb, 1985).
3   Bonaventure, from *Soul's Journey into God*, in *Classics of Western Spirituality: Bonaventure*, ed. Ewert Cousins (New York: Paulist Press, 1978).
4   Nuala O'Faoláin, *Are You Somebody?* (Dublin: New Island Books, Irish Books & Media, Inc., 1996), p. 9.
5   Ibid., pp. 11, 112-13.
6   Henri J. M. Nouwen, *The Return of the Prodigal Son: A Story of Homecoming* (New York: Image Books, Doubleday, 1992), pp. 106-9.
7   Rudyard Kipling.
8   Ellen Gregory, 'Angels and the Apocalypse: Hilda Doolittle's Tribute to the Angels', in *The Angels,* ed. Robert Sardello (New York: Continuum, 1994), p. 148.
9   Ibid.
10   Webb Garrison, *Creative Imagination in Preaching*.
11   Sr Frances Theresa OSC, *Living the Incarnation* (Quincy, IL: Franciscan Press, 1996), p. 51.

12   Henri J. M. Nouwen, Donald P. Neill and Douglas A. Morrison, *Compassion* (London: Darton, Longman and Todd, 1982), p. 20.

13   Armstrong and Brady, *Francis and Clare*, Admonition V, p. 29.

14   Ibid., p. 26.

15   Ibid., p. 67.

16   Ibid., p. 83.

17   Ibid., p. 94.

18   Ibid., p. 57.

19   Cf. *Studia Mystica*, V1118, 2 (Summer 1985); pp. 4-14, p. 5.

20   Columbas Stewart, 'Radical Honesty About the Self: The Practice of the Desert Fathers', *Sobornost* (12 January 1990), p. 25.

21   Ibid., p. 27.

22   Ibid., p. 28.

23   Ibid., p. 29.

24   Gustave Gutierrez, *Theology of Liberation* (Maryknoll, New York: Orbis Books, 1988), pp. 116-20.

25   Habig, *Omnibus of Sources,* 2 Cel. 4, p. 364.

26   Ibid., Legend of the Three Companions 2-4, p. 893.

27   Ibid., p. 364.

28   Armstrong/Hellman/Short, *Francis of Assisi,* vol. 1, ch. 2, 3-4, pp. 184-5.

29   Habig, *Omnibus of Sources,* LM, ch. 2, pp. 636-7.

30   Armstrong/Hellman/Short, *Francis of Assisi,* ch. 2, 4-5, p. 187.

31   Ibid., ch. 3, 6, p. 187.

32   Ibid., ch. 3, 7, p. 188.

33   Habig, *Omnibus of Sources,* L3C, ch. 2, 5 and 6, pp. 894-5.

34   Ibid., LM, ch. 1:3, pp. 637-8.

35   Ibid., L3C, ch. IV, p. 901.

36   Ibid., ch. V, pp. 903-4.

37   Ibid., L3C, ch. VII. 17, pp. 242-3.

38   Ibid., 1 Cel, ch. IX, 9:21-22, pp. 246-7.

39   Ibid., L3C, ch. 8: 27-28, pp. 916-7.

40   Ibid., 2 Cel, 209, p. 529.

41   Ibid., ch. 10, 36, p. 925.

42   Jacques de Vitry, quoted by Raoul Manselli, *St Francis of Assisi* (Quincy, IL: Franciscan Press, 1988), p. 220.

43   Ibid., pp 220-21.

44 Ibid.
45 Habig, *Omnibus of Sources*, 13th-Century Testimonies, Verba Illuminati, pp. 1614-15.
46 Habig, *Omnibus of Sources*, Little Flowers of St Francis, ch. 21, p. 1348.
47 Ibid., pp. 1348-50.
48 Armstrong and Brady, *Francis and Clare*, pp. 99-100.
49 Armstrong/Hellman/Short, *Francis of Assisi*, 1 Cel 2:92, p. 262.
50 Ibid., 2 Cel, ch. LXI, 95, p. 440.
51 Norbert Nguyen Van-Khanh OFM, *The Teacher of His Heart: Jesus Christ in the Thoughts and Writings of St Francis*, Franciscan Pathways (New York: The Franciscan Institute, 1994), p. 223.
52 Regis J. Armstrong, *St Francis of Assisi: Writings for a Gospel Life* (New York: Crossroads, 1994), p. 238.
53 Raoul Manselli, *St Francis of Assisi* (Quincy, IL: Franciscan Press, 1988) pp. 159-60.
54 Ibid., p. 160.
55 Ibid.
56 Ibid., p. 161.
57 Ibid., pp. 162-3.
58 Ibid., p. 161.
59 Regis J. Armstrong OFMCap, *Clare of Assisi*, p. 276.
60 Ibid., p. 277.
61 Ibid.
62 Ibid.
63 Ibid., pp. 277-8.
64 Marco Bartoli, *Clare of Assisi* (Quincy, IL: Franciscan Press, 1993), p. 170.
65 Ibid., p. 173.
66 Ibid., pp. 96-7.

Resources: Sisterhood and Brotherhood

1 Bonaventure, *Soul's Journey*, Prologue.
2 Armstrong and Brady, *Francis and Clare*, 1 L. Ag., pp. 15-18.
3 William R. Cook, *Francis of Assisi* (MGP, Liturgical Press, 1989), pp. 36, 37.

4   Armstrong and Brady, *Francis and Clare*, The Earlier Rule, ch. 9, verse 2, p. 117.
5   Saul Nathanial Brody, *The Disease of the Soul: Leprosy in Medieval Literature* (Ithaca & London: Cornell University Press 1974), p. 147.
6   Ibid., pp. 129-30.
7   Ibid., pp. 130-31.
8   Ibid., pp. 131-32.
9   Ibid., pp. 60-61.
10 Ibid., p. 61.
11 Ibid., p. 64.
12 Ibid., p. 65.
13 Ibid., pp. 66-67 (punctuation modified).
14 Ibid., p. 68.
15 Ibid., pp. 68-9.
16 Ibid., p. 69.
17 Ibid., p. 73.
18 Ibid., pp. 73-4.
19 Ibid., p. 74.
20 Ibid., p. 75.
21 Ibid., p. 83.
22 Ibid., p. 86.
23 Gerald G. May, *Addiction and Grace* (New York: HarperCollins, 1991), p. 144.
24 Frances Theresa OSC, *Living the Incarnation* (Quincy, IL: Franciscan Press, 1996), pp. 51-2.
25 Frank O'Connor, *My Father's Son* (Belfast: The Blackstaff Press, 1994), p. 79.
26 *We Were With St Francis: The Legend of the Three Companions*, trans. Salvator Butler OFM (Edizioni Porziuncola: 1984), p. 126.
27 Frances Theresa OSC, *Living the Incarnation* (Quincy, IL: Franciscan Press), pp. 53-4.
28 Armstrong/Hellman/Short, *Francis of Assisi*, p. 103.
29 Henri J. M. Nouwen, *Prodigal Son*, p. 121.
30 Ibid., p. 129.
31 Ibid.

32   Ibid., pp. 130-31.

33   Ibid., pp. 131-33.

34   Ibid., pp. 138-9.

35   R. R. Ruether, *Sexism and God Talk* (Crossroad Publishing Co. and SCM Press, 1983), p. 137.

36   Armstrong and Brady, *Francis and Clare,* Fourth Letter to Blessed Agnes of Prague, pp. 204-5.

37   Armstrong, *Clare of Assisi,* pp. 50-51.

38   Armstrong, *Clare of Assisi,* Fourth Letter to Blessed Agnes of Prague, p. 205.

39   Ruth Page, *The Incarnation of Freedom and Love* (Cleveland, Ohio: Pilgrim Press), pp. 163-4.

40   Gerald G. May MD, *Addiction and Grace: Love and Spirituality in the Healing of Addictions* (San Francisco: Harper Collins), pp. 135-6.

41   Mother Theresa, *My Life with the Poor,* ed. Jose Luiz Gonzales and Janet N. Playfoot (San Francisco: Harper & Row, 1995), pp. 96-100.

42   *San Francisco Chronicle.*

43   *Sympathetic Vibration,* K. C. Cole.

44   R. S. Thomas, *Collective Poems 1945-1990* (London: J. M. Dent, 1993).

45   Alexander Schemenmann, *For the Life of the World: Sacraments and Orthodoxy* (St Vladimir's Seminary Press, 1973).

46   Carol Ann Duffy, b. 1955.

47   Timothy Johnson OFMConv., 'Image and Vision: Contemplation as Visual Perception in Clare of Assisi's Epistolary Writings', *Greyfriars Review,* vol. 8, no. 2 (1994), p. 205.

48   Old Sanskrit proverb.

49   Henri Nouwen, *With Burning Hearts* (Maryknoll, New York: Orbis Books, 1994), pp. 94-5.

50   Ibid., pp. 84-5.

Resources: Peace

1   At Drogheda, Ireland, 1979.

2   Armstrong and Brady, *Francis and Clare,* The Salutation of the Virtues, 9, p. 152.

3   Ibid.
4   Ibid.
5   Bonaventure, *Breviloquium*, V.1, p. 184.
6   E. N. Maclaren.
7   Zachary Hayes, *The Hidden Center* (New York: Paulist Press, 1991), p. 61.
8   Ibid., pp. 136-7.
9   Margaret Eletta Guider OSF, 'Foundations for a Theology of Presence (a consideration of the Scotist understanding of the primary purpose of the Incarnation and its relevance for ministry in the underworld of the world church)', *The Cord: A Franciscan Spiritual Review* (20 March 1993), p. 77.
10   *Evangelium Vitae*, an encyclical by Pope John Paul II, no. 87 (Dublin: Veritas) p. 154.
11   Benet A. Fonck OFM, *Fully Mature with the Fullness of Christ* (Chicago: Franciscan Province of the Sacred Heart), ch. 7, ch. 39.
12   Octavian Schmucki OFM, 'Initiation into the Franciscan Life – Early Sources', *Greyfriars Review*, vol 2 (June 1988), p. 7.
13   Brody, *The Disease of the Soul*, pp. 102-3.
14   Ibid., p. 103.
15   Ibid., p. 104.
16   Ibid., pp. 104-5.
17   Armstrong/Hellman/Short, *Francis of Assisi*, vol. 1, 101, p. 271.
18   Octavian Schmucki OFM, 'The Illnesses of Francis During the Last Years of His Life', *Greyfriars Review*, vol. 13, no. 1 (1999), p. 7.
19   Armstrong and Brady, *Francis and Clare*, The Earlier Rule (RNB), ch. 12.
20   Ibid., p. 120.
21   Armstrong and Brady, *Francis and Clare*, Preachers, ch. IX, p. 143.
22   Frances Theresa OSC, *Living the Incarnation* (Quincy, IL: Franciscan Press), p. 128.
23   Salle McFague, *The Body of God: An Ecological Theology* (SCM Press), p. 212, citing Julian of Norwich, modernised from *A Revelation of Love*, ed. Marian Glasscoe (Exeter: University of Exeter Press, 1988), ch. 5.

24 Alice Walker, 'The Gospel According to Shug', in *The Temple of My Familiar* (New York: Simon and Schuster, 1989), pp. 288-9.

25 Gerald G. May, *Addiction and Grace* (Harper Collins, 1991), p. 137.

26 Gerald G. May, 'Deliverance', in *Addiction and Grace*, pp. 152-3.

27 Ibid., pp. 157-60.

28 Ibid., p. 160.

29 Ibid., pp. 160-61.

30 Ibid.

31 Ibid., p. 181.

32 Hanbury Brown, *The Wisdom of Science: Its Relevance to Culture and Religion* (Cambridge: Cambridge University Press, 1986), p. 172.

33 Ibid., p. 167.

34 Cf. Clare's death in Armstrong, *Clare of Assisi*, pp. 228-9 and *Living the Incarnation,* Frances Teresa OSC, pp. 111-12.

35 Julio Mico, *Greyfriars Review,* VIII: 3 (1994), p. 270.

36 Ibid., p. 167.

37 Armstrong and Brady, *Francis and Clare*, p. 196.

38 Julio Mico, 'The Spirit of Saint Francis: The Gospel Life', *Greyfriars Review,* VII: 3 (1994), p. 298.

39 John Bell (b. 1949) and Graham Maule (b. 1958), Hymn No. 70, (Iona Community, Wildgoose Publishers, 1987).

40 Lester Brown, Worldwatch Institute President, 'Crossing the Threshold: Early Signs of an Environmental Awakening', *World Watch* (March/April, 1999).

41 Report of the Secretary General of the UN, 1997.

42 EPA Report, *State of the Environment in Ireland,* 1996.

43 *Human Development Index,* a Report by the UN Development Programme, 1998.

44 Antoine de St Exupery, *The Little Prince* (London: Mammoth, 1991), p. 16.

45 Blaise Pascal, *The Pensees,* trans. J. M. Cohen (Baltimore: Penguin, 1961), p. 96.

46 *Centesimus Annus* (100th anniversary of *Rerum Novarum*), No. 37, Pope John Paul II.

47 *The World Day of Peace: The Ecological Crisis. A Common Responsibility,* Pope John Paul II.

48   Jerome Poulenc, 'The Modern Inspiration for the Prayer, "Lord, Make Me an Instrument of Your Peace"', *Greyfriars Review*, vol. 10, no. 3 (1996), p. 268.
49   Habig, *Omnibus of Sources*, Mirror of Perfection, 101, p. 1237.
50   Armstrong/Hellman/Short, *Francis of Assisi*, vol. 1, p. 114.
51   Regis J. Armstrong, *St Francis of Assisi: Writings for a Gospel Life* (New York, Crossroad, 1994), pp. 208-9.
52   Ibid., p. 212.
53   Ibid., p. 238.

Epilogue

1   *Gaudium et Spes*, Vatican II, 38.
2   Whitehand, *Religion in the Making* (New York: The Start Company, 1926), p. 115.
3   Piet Schoonenberg SJ, 'I Believe in Eternal Life', in *Concilium Dogma: the Problem of Eschatology* (New York: Glen Rock, NJ, 1960), p. 110.
4   Theodosius Foley OFMCap, *In the Spirit of St Francis* (St Anthony Guild Press, 1949), p. 138.
5   Armstrong and Brady, *Francis of Assisi*, RB, ch. vi, p. 141.
6   Leonardo Boff, *Saint Francis* (London: SCM Press Ltd, 1986), p. 134.
7   Zachary Hayes OFM, *A Window to the Divine* (Quincy, IL: Franciscan Press, 1997), p. 82.
8   Ernest Raymond, *In the Steps of St Francis* (Quincy, IL: Franciscan Press, 1970).

BIBLIOGRAPHY

Armstrong, Regis J., OFMCap, *Saint Francis of Assisi: Writings for a Gospel Life* (New York: Crossroad Publishing Company, 1994).

—— *Clare of Assisi, Early Documents* (revised and expanded), (New York: Franciscan Institute Publications, Saint Bonaventure University, 1993).

Armstrong, Regis and Ignatius Brady, *Francis and Clare: The Complete Works* (New York: Paulist Press, 1982).

Armstrong, Regis J., OFMCap, J. A. Wayne OFMConv, and William J. Short OFM, *Francis of Assisi: Early Documents*, vol. 1, *The Saint* (New York: New City Press, 1999).

Bartoli, Marco, *Clare of Assisi* (Quincy, IL: Franciscan Press, 1993).

Bauer, Francis, *Life in Abundance* (New York: Paulist Press, 1993).

Benet, A., OFM, *Fully Mature with the Fullness of Christ* (3rd Edition), (Chicago: Franciscan Province of the Sacred Heart).

Bezunarta, Jesus-Maria, OFMCap, 'Clare of Assisi and the Discernment of Spirits', *Greyfriars Review*, Supplement 8, 1994.

Bodo, Murray, OFM, *Tales of Saint Francis: Ancient Stories for Contemporary Living* (New York: Doubleday, 1988).

Borg, Marcus, *Meeting Jesus Again for the First Time* (San Francisco: Harper, 1994).

Brody, Saul Nathaniel, *The Disease of the Soul: Leprosy in Medieval Literature* (Ithaca & London: Cornell University Press, 1974).

Brown, Hanbery, *The Wisdom of Science: Its Relevance to Culture and Religion* (Cambridge: Cambridge University Press, 1986).

Butler, Salvator, OFM (trans.), *We Were With Saint Francis: The Legend of the Three Companions* (Edizione Porziuncula, 1984).

Byron, William J., SJ, 'Discernment in Poverty', *The Way*, Supplement 23 (1974), pp. 37-42.

Canonici, Luciano, 'Leper, Leprosarium', *Greyfriars Review*, vol. 9, no. 3 (1995), pp. 251, 257.

Carney, Margaret, OSF, *The First Franciscan Woman: Clare of Assisi and Her Form of Life* (Quincy, Illinois: Franciscan Press, 1993).

Chesterton, G. K., *Saint Francis of Assisi* (New York: Image Books, Doubleday, 1957).

Cirino, André, OFM, and Raischl, Josef, (eds), *Franciscan Solitude* (New York: Franciscan Institute, 1994).

Columbus, Stewart, 'Radical Honesty About the Self: The Practice of the Desert Fathers', *Sobornost*, 1-12 (1990), p. 25.

Cook, William R., *Francis of Assisi, The Way of the Christian Mystic* (Collegeville, Minnesota: Michael Glazier Books, 1989).

Cousins, Ewert H., *Bonaventure, The Classics of Western Spirituality* (New York: Paulist Press, 1978).

Day, Dorothy, *Loaves and Fishes* (Maryknoll, New York: Orbis Books, 1997).

DeLaBedoyere, Michael, *Francis: A Biography of the Saint of Assisi* (London: Collins, 1962).

Doyle, Eric, OFM, *Saint Francis and the Song of Brotherhood and Sisterhood* (New York: Franciscan Institute, 1997).

Esser, Cajetan, OFM, *Origins of the Franciscan Order* (Quincy, IL: Franciscan Press, 1970).

Flood, David, OFM and Thadee Matura, OFM, *The Birth of a Movement: A Study of the First Rule of Saint Francis* (Quincy, IL: Franciscan Press, 1975).

Fortini, Arnaldo, *Francis of Assisi* (New York: Crossroad Publishing Company, 1980).

Frankl, Viktor E., *Man's Search for Meaning* (New York: Pocket Books, 1963).

Frugoni, Chiara, *Francis of Assisi* (London: SCM Press Ltd, 1998).

Gollwitzer, Helmut, *The Way to Life, Sermons in a Time of World Crisis* (Edinburgh: T. & T. Clark, 1981).

Grundmann, Herbert, *Religious Movements in the Middle Ages* (Notre Dame, Illinois: University of Notre Dame Press, 1995).

Guinan, Michael, *To Be Human Before God* (Collegeville, Minnesota: The Liturgical Press, 1994).

Habig, Marion A., (ed.), *Saint Francis of Assisi, Omnibus of Sources* (Quincy, IL: Franciscan Press, 1973).

Hayes, Zachary, OFM, *The Hidden Center: Spirituality and Speculative Christology in St Bonaventure* (New York: Paulist Press, 1991).

Hone, Mary Francis, OSC (ed.) Clare Centenary Series: An Eight Volume Series in Honor of the Birth of Saint Clare, vols. I-IV: *Toward the Discovery of Clare of Assisi;* vol. V: *A Biographical Guide to Saint Clare of Assisi and Her Order;* vol. VII: *Clare of Assisi, A Medieval and Modern Woman;* vol. VIII: *Clare, Selected Papers* (New York: Franciscan Institute, Bonaventure University, 1996).

Hugo, William R., OFMCap., *A Study in the Life of Francis of Assisi: A Beginner's Workbook* (Quincy, IL: Franciscan Press, 1996).

Karper, Karen PCPA, *Clare: Her Light and Her Song* (Quincy, IL: Franciscan Press, 1984).

Kelly, Ignatius, 'Poverty as a Spiritual Value', *The Way*, Supplement 80 (1994), pp. 25-32.

La Conversione alla Poverta, Nell'Italia Dei Secoli, XII to XIV, Nuova Serie Diretta Da Enrico Menesto (Spoleto: Centro Italiano de Studi Sull'alto Medioevo Spoleto, Academia Tudertina, 1991).

LeGoff, Jacques, *Medieval Civilization, 400 to 1500* (Cambridge, MA: Blackwell Limited, 1988).

Manselli, Raoul, *Saint Francis of Assisi* (Chicago, IL: Franciscan Herald Press, 1988).

Matura, Thaddee, OFM, *Francis of Assisi: The Message in His Writing* (New York: Franciscan Institute Publications, 1997).

May, Gerald, *Addiction and Grace* (New York: Harper Collins, 1991).

McElrath, Damian, *Franciscan Christology*, Franciscan Resources no. 1, (New York: Franciscan Institute Publications, 1994).

Moorman, John R. H., *Saint Francis of Assisi* (London: SPCK Publishers, 1963).

Nasali-Rocca, Emilio, 'Gli Ospedali Italiani di S. Lazzaro, O Dei Lebbrosi', *ZRG Kapt*, vol. 27, (1938), pp. 262-9.

Nouwen, Henri, *The Return of the Prodigal Son: A Story of Homecoming* (New York: Image Books, Doubleday, 1998).

—— *With Burning Hearts* (Maryknoll, New York: Orbis, 1994).

O'Donohue, John, *Anam Cara: A Book of Celtic Wisdom* (New York: Harper Collins, 1997).

Osborne, Kenan, OFM (ed.) *The History of Franciscan Theology* (New York: Franciscan Institute, Bonaventure University, 1994).

Palmer, Richard, 'The Church, Leprosy and Plague', in *Studies In Church History*, vol. 19, *The Church and Healing*, Ecclesiastical History Society, Summer Meeting (Oxford: Blackwell, 1982).

Peterson, Ingrid J., OSF, *Clare of Assisi: A Biographical Study* (Quincy, IL: Franciscan Press, 1993).

Raymond, Ernest, *In The Steps of Saint Francis* (Quincy, IL: Franciscan Press, 1970).

Rossiaud, Jacques, *Medieval Prostitution* (Cambridge, MA: Blackwell).

Shea, John, *Stories of Faith* (Chicago, IL: Thomas More Press, 1980).

Short, William, *The Franciscans* (Collegeville, Minnesota: Liturgical Press, 1989).

Smolinski, Arcadius, 'The Spirit of Prayer in Work', *The Cord*, vol. 118, no. 2 (November 1958), pp. 344-9.

Theresa, Sister Frances, *Living the Incarnation* (Quincy, IL: Franciscan Press, 1996).

Underhill, Evelyn, *Practical Mysticism* (New York: Dutton, 1943).

Van Asseldonk, Optatus, OFMCap, 'The Holy Spirit in the Life and Writings of Saint Clare', *Greyfriars Review*, no. 1 (1987), pp. 93-104.

—— 'Life in the Whole Unity, According to Saint Francis and Saint Clare', *The Cord*, no. 42 (1991), pp. 205-22.

—— 'The Spirit of the Lord and its Holy Activity in the Writings of Francis', *Greyfriars Review*, no. 5 (1991), pp. 105-58.

Vanier, Jean, *Be Not Afraid* (Toronto: Griffin House, 1975).

Ward, Benedicta, 'Discernment: A Rare Bird', *The Way*, Supplement 64 (1989), pp. 10-18.

Weaver, Mark, OFM, Conv., 'The Testament of the Fractured Fraternity of Francis', *Greyfriars Review*, vol. 10, no. 3 (1996).

Witherup, Ronald D., *Conversion in the New Testament* (Collegeville, Minnesota: Michael Glazier Book, Liturgical Press).